ART BOOKS

FROM CRESCENT MOON PUBLISHING

Leonardo da Vinci
by James Pearson

Early Netherlandish Painting
by Rosalind Mutter

Piero della Francesca
by Naomi Haskell

Giovanni Bellini
by Julia Davis

Fra Angelico: Art and Religion in the Renaissance
by Rosalind Mutter

Eric Gill: Nuptials of God
by Anthony Hoyland

Minimal Art and Artists in the 1960s and After
by Laura Garrard

Postwar Art
by George Knighton

Vincent van Gogh: Visionary Landscapes
by Stuart Morris

Max Beckmann
by Stuart Morris

Egon Schiele: Sex and Death in Purple Stockings
by D. Simon Eade

Mark Rothko: The Art of Transcendence
by Julia Davis

Jasper Johns
by L.M. Poole

Brice Marden
by Laura Garrard

Frank Stella: From Minimalism to Maximalism
by James Pearson

The Light Eternal: J.M.W. Turner
by Jeremy Mark Robinson

Maurice Sendak and the Art of Children's Book Illustration
by L.M. Poole

Sex in Art: Pornography and Pleasure in Painting and Sculpture
by Cassidy Hughes

Glorification: Religious Abstraction
in Renaissance and 20th Century Painting
by Jeremy Mark Robinson

The Art of Andy Goldsworthy
by William Malpas

The Art of Andy Goldsworthy
by William Malpas

Andy Goldsworthy: Touching Nature
by William Malpas

Andy Goldsworthy In Close-Up
by William Malpas

The Art of Richard Long
by William Malpas

Constantin Brancusi: Sculpting the Essence of Things
by James Pearson

Alison Wilding: The Embrace of Sculpture
by Susan Quinnell

The Erotic Object: Sexuality in Sculpture
From Prehistory to the Present Day
by Susan Quinnell

Land Art, Earthworks, Installations, Environments, Sculpture
by William Malpas

Land Art: A Complete Guide to Landscape, Environmental,
Earthworks, Nature, Sculpture and Installation Art
by William Malpas

Richard Long In Close-Up
by William Malpas

Land Art In Close-Up
by William Malpas

*Colourfield Painting: Minimal, Cool, Hard Edge, Serial
and Post-Painterly Abstract Art From the Sixties to the Present*
by Laura Garrard

Sacred Gardens: The Garden in Myth, Religion and Art
by Jeremy Mark Robinson

FRA ANGELICO

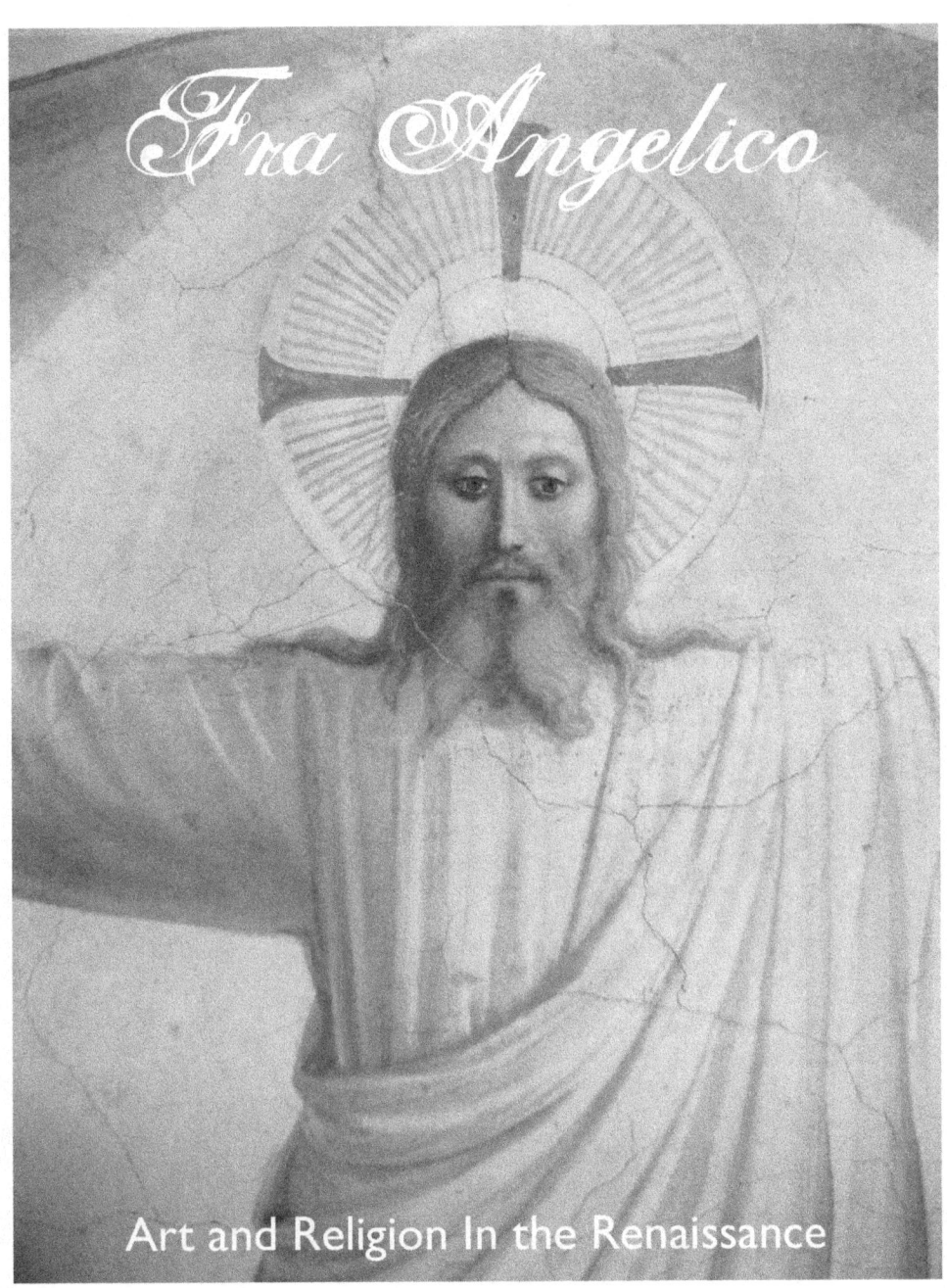

Fra Angelico

Art and Religion In the Renaissance

ROSALIND MUTTER

Crescent Moon

CRESCENT MOON PUBLISHING
P.O. Box1312, Maidstone
Kent, ME14 5XU
Great Britain

First published 1995. Second edition 2008.
© Rosalind Mutter 2008, 2018. Reprinted with revisions 2018.

Printed and bound by in the U.S.A..
Set in Book Antiqua 9 on 14pt.
Designed by Radiance Graphics.

British Library Cataloguing in Publication data

Mutter, Rosalind
Fra Angelico: Art and Religion in
the Renaissance. – (Painters Series)
I. Title II. Series

759.5

ISBN-13 9781861711625 (Pbk)
ISBN-13 9781861717566 (Pbk)
ISBN-13 9781861715685 (Hbk)

Contents

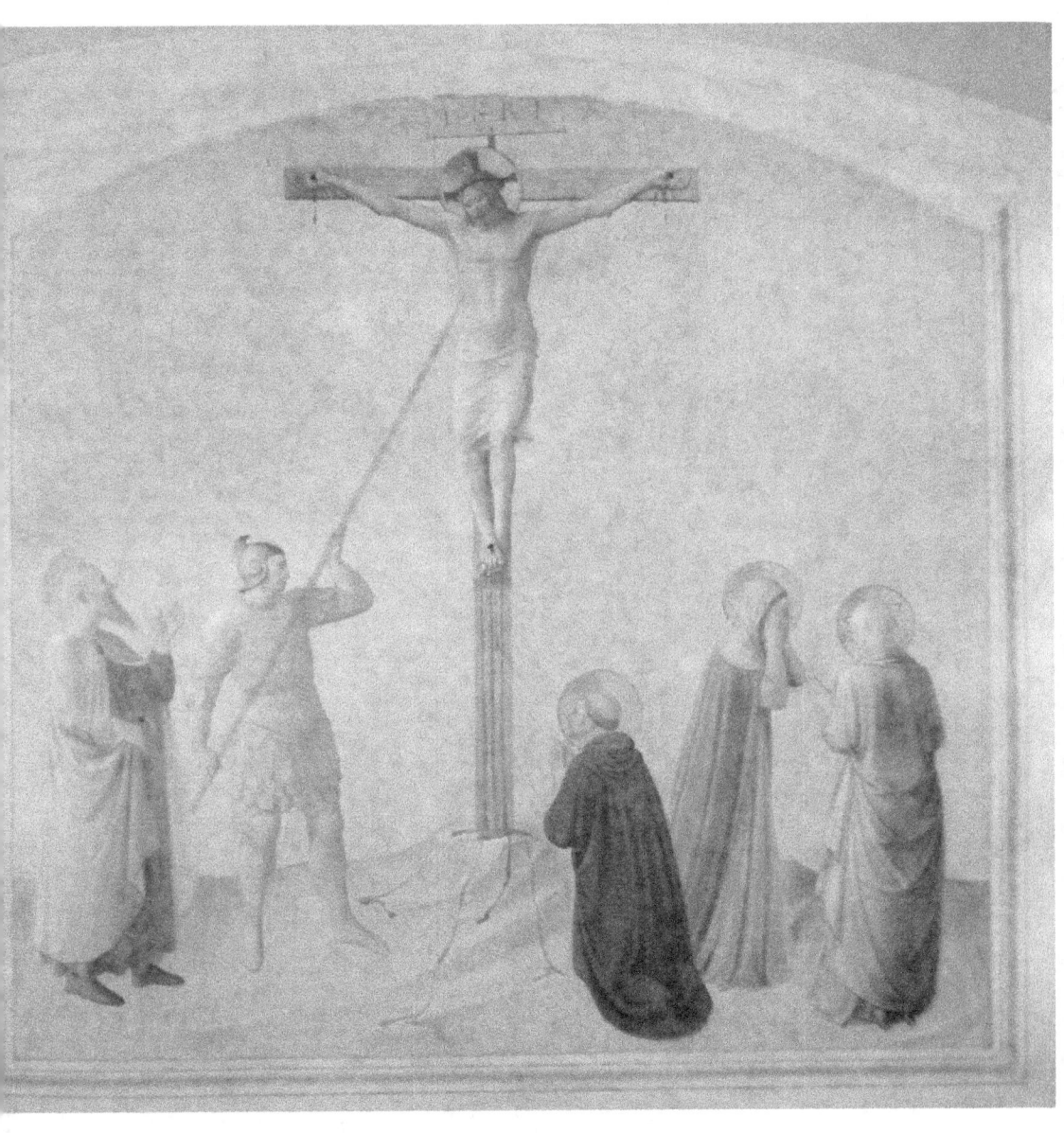

Fra Angelico, Crucifixion, cell 42, San Marco

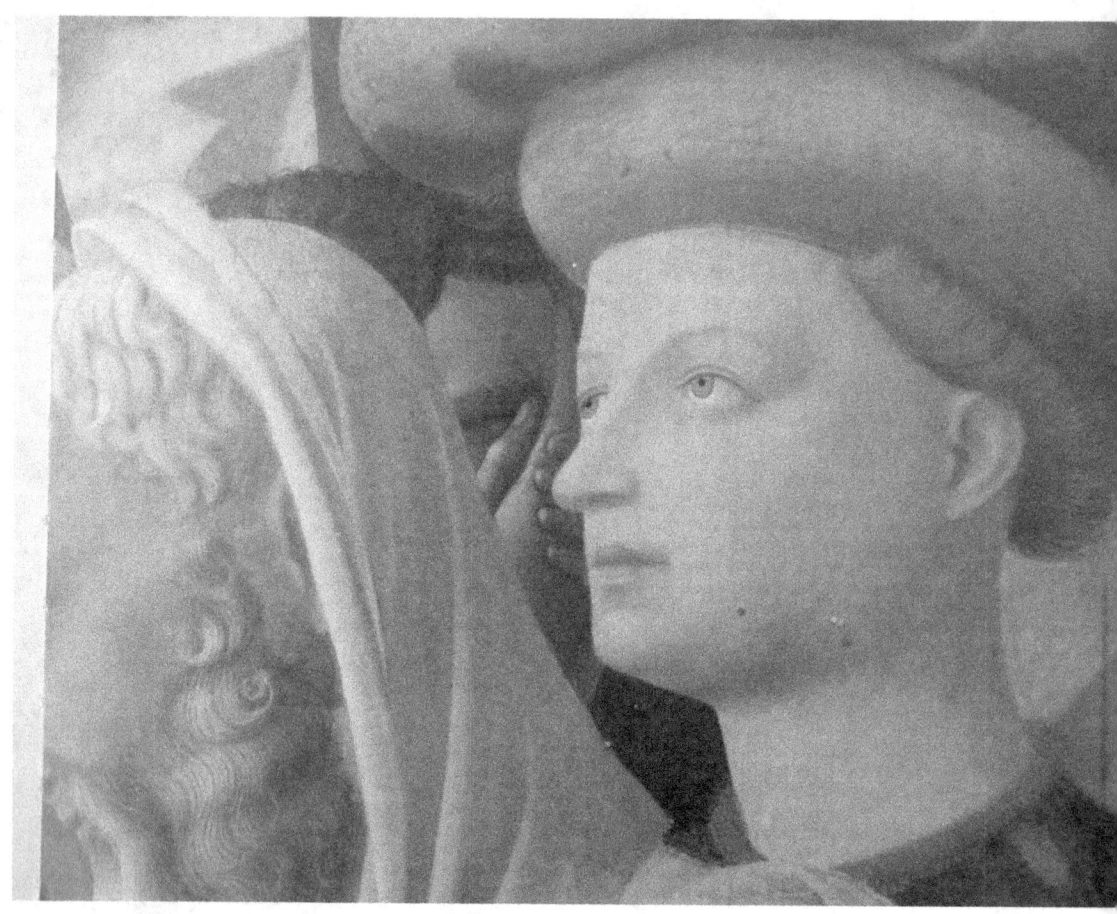

Fra Angelico, Descent From the Cross, detail, San Marco

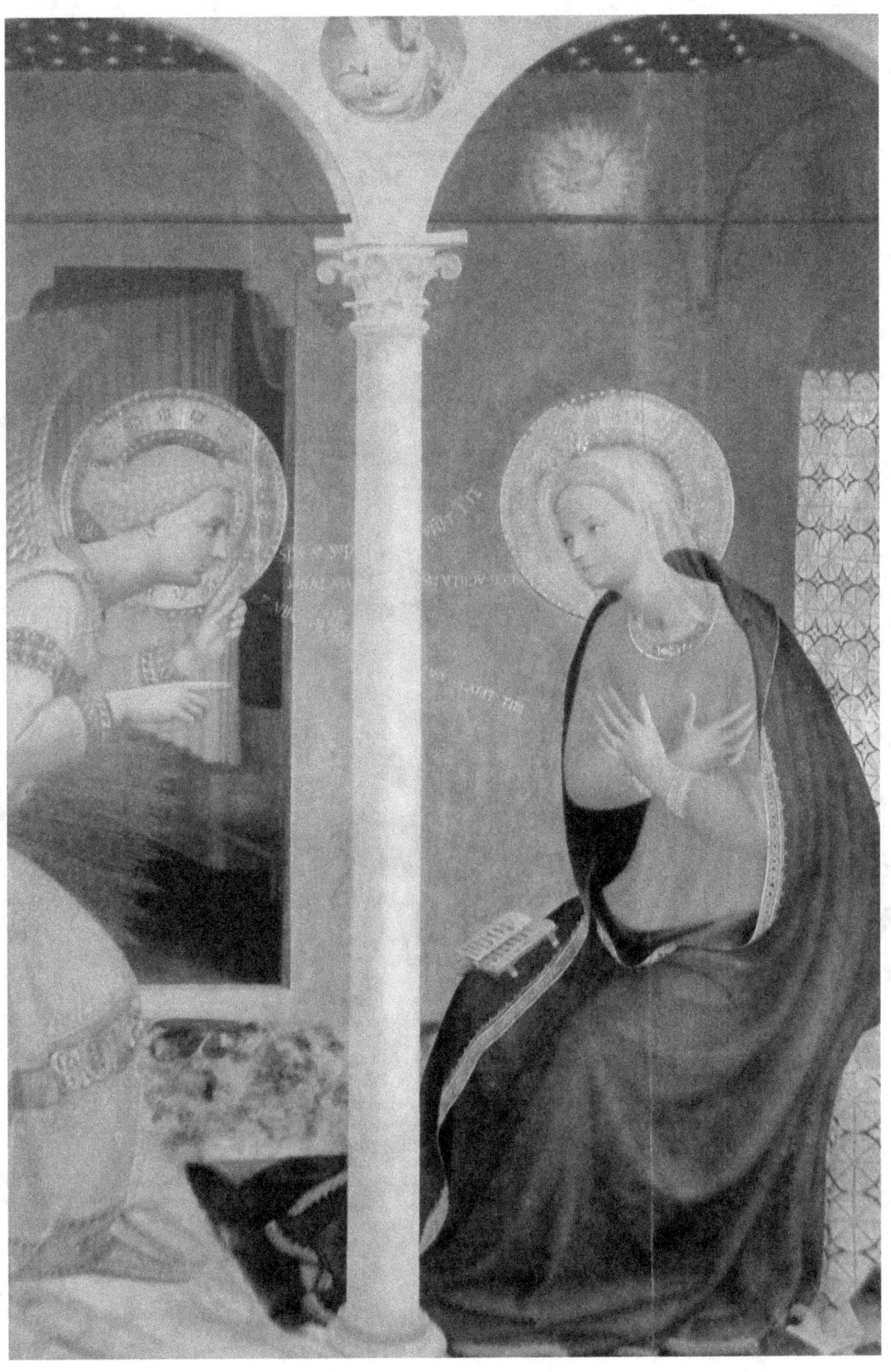

Fra Angelico, Anunciation, Cortona

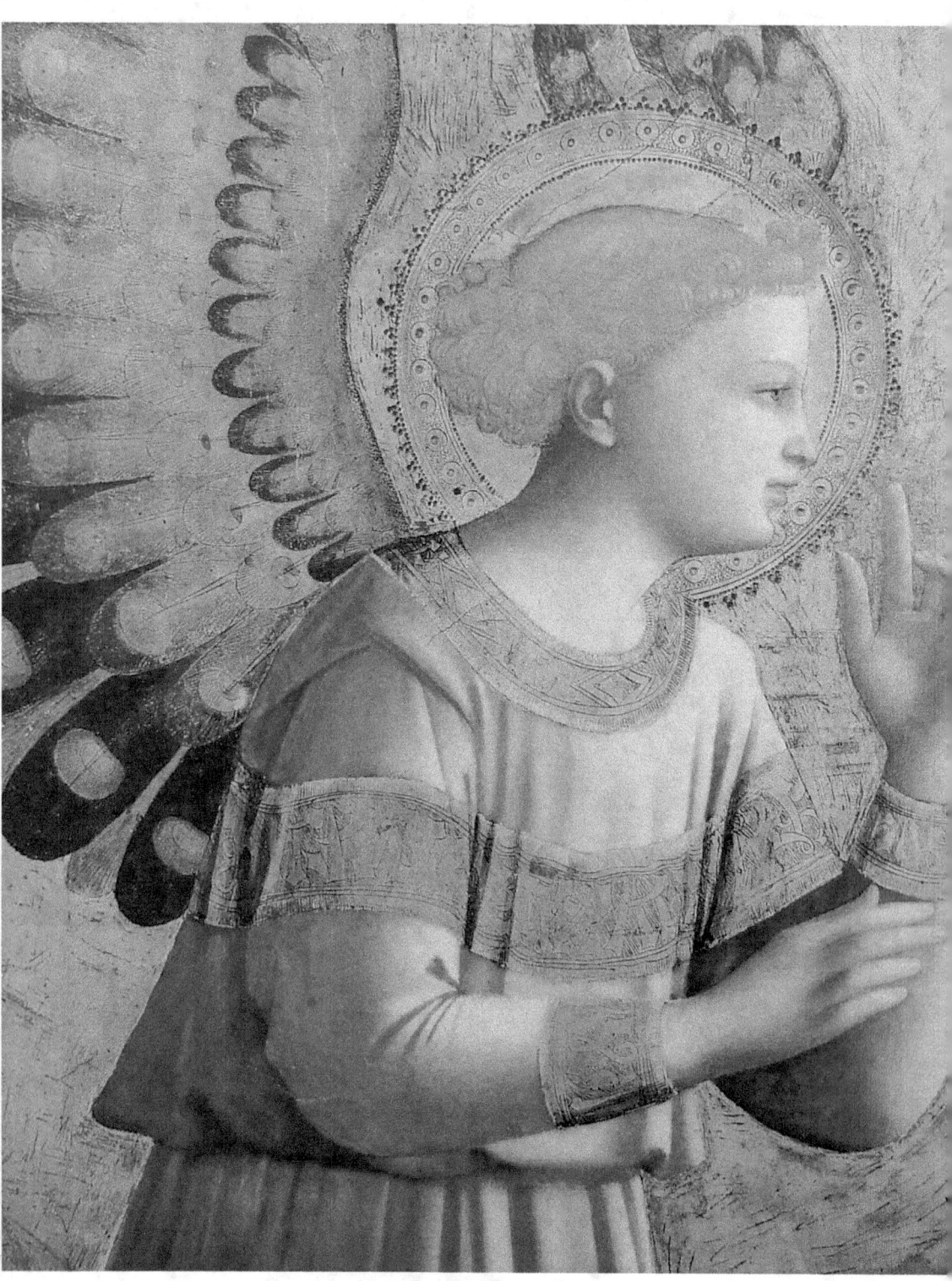

Fra Angelico, Annunciatory Angel, c. 1437-46, Detroit Institute of Arts

I

Fra Angelico and the Renaissance

FRA ANGELICO, KNOWN by different names, including Fra Giovanni Beato Angelico da Fiesole (1399?-1455), is one of the very few artists of the Italian Renaissance who painted religious pictures exclusively. Almost all Fra Angelico's paintings are religious – he did not paint secular portraits, like, say, Giovanni Bellini or Domenico Ghirlandaio.[1] It was the art impresario Giorgio Vasari who stressed Angelico's purity, holiness, faith, humility and devout nature (204f), and this description of Angelico as a holy monk-like painter persists throughout the centuries. Art critic John Ruskin called Angelico 'an inspired saint'.

It is in the Convent of San Marco in Florence that Fra Angelico's 'saintly' reputation was forged.[2] If you haven't been to San Marco, you must. It is unforgettable. Fra Angelico (with assistants) painted fifty frescoes at San Marco. The paintings reveal a traditional form of Christian (here, Catholic) worship: Angelico's is a conventional kind of Christian theology and devotion.

Some critics emphasize Fra Angelico as a stylist.[3] Of course, Angelico did not separate style from content in the way modern critics do. Clearly, they are part of the same thing. For the Renaissance religious painter, the aim is to come up with a style, coloration and technique which accords with one's beliefs, as well as flattering the faith of one's patrons. So Angelico's 'sweet style' stems from his blending of painterly technique with religious understanding. If God or the Virgin Mary are holy, they demand a holy treatment in paint. The Renaissance altarpiece had to be beautifully painted, because belief, as well as God, was itself holy. Art was to be admired, as well as God and religion. Art had to flatter the onlooker, as well as inspire her/him to faith and devotion. That is, the more gorgeous the painting, the more gorgeous was the status reflected back onto the worshipper and the patron. Many patrons glorified themselves by having themselves painted in the same pictorial space as the holy of holies, the Virgin Mary and Child. Renaissance art was made for a sophisticated mercantile class, people who knew well the value of gold, ultramarine, fur, jewels, expensive robes, all the things in the Renaissance painting. The richness of earthly goods was translated into rich spiritual wealth.

Fra Angelico's work, though, is supremely humble, superbly (and refreshingly) anti-materialistic. Of course, Angelico painted wealthy figures, crowding around the foot of the Cross, or surrounding the throne during the Coronation of the Virgin. But Angelico did not particularly flatter his patrons and audience, in the way that Raphael Sanzio or Sandro Botticelli did. Instead, and especially at San Marco's Convent, Fra Angelico forced people to focus on the fundamental experiences of Christianity: suffering, devotion, faith, purity, and altruism. In the white cells of San Marco Convent, Angelico dispenses with the flamboyant materialism of Quattrocento art, and bids onlookers to contemplate the piercing feelings of the Christian story: Christ on the Cross, Christ in Heaven, the Transfiguration, the Coronation, and the Descent from the Cross. Fra Angelico cuts through bourgeois aspects of Renaissance painting, and forces the spectator to think on the suffering of Christ. In the midst of the San Marco *Descent From the Cross*, one of Angelico's greatest works, with its rich colouring, its expensive gilded surface and frame, and the wealthy figures, is Christ's near-naked, violated body. The sense of humility and suffering is always foremost in Angelico's work. The sense of saintliness and Christian meditation surpasses lesser elements such as painterly technique (though Angelico doesn't neglect or avoid style – Angelico is in part a showman, like all great artists). Like Giotto and Duccio di Buoninsegna, Angelico cuts through the showy trappings of high art to get at the poignant emotion underneath.

✻

The selection of Fra Angelico's paintings for discussion and the emphasis on certain aspects of his art is not comprehensive. I hope it is a representative selection and discussion, however. Angelico is often portrayed as a holy artist, working somewhere between the Christian mediæval world and the new humanism of the Renaissance, an artist who simultaneously takes up mediæval Gothic and Italian Quattrocento painterly æsthetics. The portrayal of Angelico as a fervently Christian painter, a monkish (Dominican) painter who retained his religious faith and innocence to the end of his life, has become a cliché, yet it rings true if one surveys Fra Angelico's paintings. The study of Angelico's Dominican faith and its relation to the Dominican monastery of San Marco in Florence has been lucidly discussed elsewhere (in books such William Hood's admirable *Fra Angelico at San Marco*).

My discussion acknowledges the contributions of art critics such as Ernst Gombrich, Christopher Lloyd, Kenneth Clark, Bernard Berenson, Bruce Cole, John Pope-Hennessy and Jacob Burckhardt, although I depart from them at certain points. Christopher Lloyd, for example, emphasizes Fra Angelico's importance as a stylist. This is clearly crucial, but I would not privilege style over content in Fra Angelico's art. For him, if not for any other Renaissance painter, religion and religious feeling were absolutely central. Nearly all of his paintings have a religious basis or connection in one way or another. While Renaissance painters, such as Piero della Francesca, painted portraits of patrons (Piero was well-known for his paintings of Federico II of Montefelcro), Angelico is known primarily as a religious artist.

Surveying Fra Angelico's art, one is struck by the sheer number of religious works, and the enormous dedication to religious subject matter.

Crucifixion follows *Crucifixion*, and one exquisite *Madonna and Child* comes hard upon the heels of another sublime *Madonna and Child*. This is the Fra Angelico I am interested in here. There are many other aspects of Angelico's art one could discuss apart from the religious dimension: Fra Angelico's relation to painters such as Fra Filippo Lippi, Paolo Uccello, Ambrogio Lorenzetti and Masaccio; or Angelico's relation to the Flemish or Early Netherlandish painters; or Angelico's relation to his patrons; or the theological questioning in Angelico's art. Some art historians may complain that I have not considered Angelico's work in Rome, Orvieto, Perugia and other places, and have concentrated too much on Angelico's art in San Marco Monastery. This is because I regard Angelico's San Marco paintings to be central to his art and *œuvre*. Instead of discussing every painting Fra Angelico and his workshop produced, I have chosen some of the key paintings, which I think fully represent his art.

✳

Fra Angelico stands at the transition between the mediæval and Renaissance worlds. Angelico's 'feelings are in the Middle Ages', Bernard Berenson noted in *The Italian Painters of the Renaissance* (1952, 49), yet he was distinctly a Quattrocento painter, a Renaissance painter. His art combines the timelessness and rigidity of (pre-Renaissance) icon painting, where figures are caught in bright, static, hieratic motions, with the new painterly explorations (in form, colour, space) of the Quattrocento period. Fra Angelico's Madonnas are large and monumental, exuding a powerful, frontal presence, dominating the frames they stand or (more often) sit in. They have the spiritual authority of ancient kings and deities. The Madonnas on their ornate thrones position the viewer instantly in a posture of obeisance. They command the viewer to get down on bended knee.

At the same time, the severity found in Byzantine and Greek icon paintings is modulated in Fra Angelico's art by an extraordinary tenderness and empathy. The religious intensity is softened. In amongst the artistic austerity and didacticism, there is a soft purity. Though Angelico's paintings, such as *The Virgin and Child Enthroned* in Perugia and the Cortona *Virgin and Child*, have the simplicity and directness of icons, they are executed in a fluid 15th century style. The aim is the same as with icons, however: a Christocentric contemplation.

Fra Angelico's paintings seem simple, but their simplicity is deceptive: they are the products of training and exceptional skill. Giulio Carlo Argan reminds us (in *The Renaissance*) that '[e]verything points to Fra Angelico's being in touch with the most advanced artists of his early day' (18). The deep spiritual feeling and tenderness of Fra Angelico's art seems 'simple' or 'innocent'. It does not appear cynical and world-weary. Yes, but the simplicity is not so much childish as child-like, as a regaining of the freshness of the spirit of childhood. A reactivation of the maternal realm, perhaps, which Fra Angelico manages to accomplish with a directness most other painters are incapable of reproducing.

✳

Fra Angelico's use of gold, as with the art of Early Renaissance painters such as Simone Martini or Duccio di Buoninsegna, recalls the Byzantine painters whose profuse use of gold is hardly surpassed anywhere. The richness of the gilding is intoxicating, as in ancient Egyptian jewellery (think of those solid gold pharaohs' coffins). As in Byzantine icons, the gold promotes a spiritual intensity. It is so rich, it marks off the object, whether king's mask or church altarpiece, from all other objects. Gold makes the object automatically special, different, other-worldly. Oswald Spengler noted (in *The Decline of the West*) how gold is not seen in everyday life.[4] As a non-pigment, gold is the richest and most expensive material a Renaissance painter could use. In Byzantiine icons, gold creates a sense of unearthly power, as if it is emanating from some other-wordly source, such as that common metaphor for royalty and divine power, the sun.

Fra Angelico produced one of his richest images with the Uffizi *Coronation of the Virgin* (1432). It is a panel dominated by gold, with gold being the primary visual device. The gold is scored and punched. There are many lines patterned in the gold surface, while, as usual in Quattrocento paintings, the haloes of the saints are decorated with holes. The shape of the kings' crowns are also punched out of the gold, so that there is a direct continuity between the material used in a real king's crown, and the materials employed to make the painting. As with paintings by Cimabue, Duccio di Buoninsegna (the *Maesta*, 1308-11) and Giotto (his unusual *Epiphany, c.* 1320), Angelico's *Coronation of the Virgin* trades on the precious nature of the very materials used in the artwork.[5]

Fra Angelico's *Coronation of the Virgin* image depicts one of the most triumphant moments in the Christian story, where Christ crowns His Mother and spiritual spouse. It is a moment of pure glory (though not untinged by melancholy and regret). So, Angelico piles on the gold: gold shafts of light radiate out from the central epiphany. Great spikes of light are thrown upwards, and also burst through the cloud upon which the Virgin and Christ sit. Below, angels play harps and viols, with more angels trumpeting fanfares with impossibly long instruments. *The Coronation of the Virgin* is one of Angelico's paintings of festive majesty: he moved between these large, processional and densely populated images and quiet, still scenes involving just one or two figures.

II

Fra Angelico as a Painter

THE 'LUMINOSITY' OF Fra Giovanni Beato Angelico da Fiesole's paintings, to use Julia Kristeva's term, is one of its most celebrated aspects. Angelico, as we have said, worked in a transition period, when the mediæval world became the Renaissance world. In Angelico's art we see mediæval art and religion turning into Renaissance art and religion. The religious severity and emotional distance of the Byzantine icon is softened into a human-ized, human-scale form of sacred painting. Instead of the aloof, stern faces of icon paintings, we find the faces of flesh and blood individuals.

In Fra Angelico's art, we see the gradual change from the gold back-ground of Byzantine and Trecento painting to a more 'naturalistic' Quattrocento blue sky and landscape. The gold of Heaven in Byzantine icons becomes the blue of the sky in Renaissance art. The Madonna takes part in this symbolic transformation, for She wears the sky on Her body, as C.G. Jung notes,[1] the connections between the Madonna and azure goes back a long way – to ancient Goddesses such as Isis, to the notion of the Night, the Milky Way, as a Goddess (see Erich Neumann, 224). Madonna blue persisted for a long time in Western art,[2] and azure was of course an expensive pigment (indeed, it was as expensive as gold).

Fra Angelico's paintings are full of this rich blue, which is often set directly next to bright red. At the centre of paintings such as *The Madonna of Humility with Child and Angels* and the *San Marco Altarpiece*, the colours of the Madonna's robes dominate: the crimson and the blue announce Her spiritual richness. As the punched and patterned gold of Early Renaissance and Trecento art of the backgrounds was replaced by more 'naturalistic' colours (greens, blues, browns), the work of spiritual connotation was done by the æthereal azure of the sky, and of the Virgin's cloak. But even as Renaissance art became increasingly 'realistic', with its illusions of three-dimensional space, it did not lose its 'unreality', its idealistic views of divinity, its idealizations of life (J. Kristeva, 1986, 262).

Fra Angelico's colours come from the purity of Trecento and early Quattrocento colours, where blues and reds were pure blues and pure reds, and had little or no other colours added to them, as in Simone Martini's *The Entombment* (1315, Berlin). Angelico's colours are symbolic and ideal, not obviously 'naturalistic' in a post-Renaissance manner, not like Paolo Veronese or Rembrandt van Rijn. In Fra Angelico's paintings, the saturation of naturalistic colour does the work of gold in Byzantine icons: to emphasize the specialness of divinity. Tonally, Angelico's paintings are generally light. He prefers a relatively uncomplicated tonal background upon which to place his figures. The San Marco frescoes are marked by a sparse white background upon which the religious figures glow. Angelico does paint shadows in the folds of costumes. No Renaissance painter could ignore carefully crafted shadows and folds. Angelico, though, keeps to soft, light greys in the folds, as also in the art of Piero della Francesca, Sassetta and Masaccio. Compared to the Early Netherlandish painters (the van Eycks, Rogier van der Weyden, Hans Memling, Quentin Massys, Gerard David, Petrus Christus *et al*), Angelico's art is very light and ideal. Even though they employ dark tones at times, the Quattrocento painters (Masaccio, Angelico, Masolino da Panicale, Antonio Pisanello, Gentile da Fabriano, Sassetta, Domenico Vaneziano), are all tonally bright.

III

The Silent Annunciation

Gegrüßt sei, meine Seele sieht:
du bist bereit und reifst.
Du bist ein großes, hohes Tor,
un aufgehn wirst du bald.
Du, meines Liedes libstes Ohr,
jetzt fühle ich: mein Wort verlor
sich in dir wie im Wald.

Rainer Maria Rilke, 'Annunciation. The Words of the Angel'[1]

ONE OF FRA Beato Angelico da Fiesole's specialties in painting was the Annunciation of the Archangel Gabriel carrying the Word of God and the Holy Spirit to the Virgin Mary, the 'handmaid of the Lord' (J. Cartwright, 104). In his *Annunciations* Fra Angelico created his most poignant meditations on spirituality in action. But the action is muted, soft, silent and tranquil.

The Annunciation expresses an important doctrinal point in mediæval Christian thought. It stressed the Virgin's total lack of sexual relations, Her purity and perfection, views which Catholics still hold (Geoffrey

Ashe, 63). The Angel Gabriel greets Mary with the words *Ave Maria, gratia plena* – 'hail Mary, full of grace'. She answers *Ecce Ancilla Domina* – 'Behold, the handmaid of the Lord' (J. Metford, 13). She is usually found reading (*Isaiah*, 7:14). The Archangel often carries a lily, or lilies are seen in the picture – a symbol of the Virgin's purity. Light streams in through a window, traditionally symbolizing virginity, but also mythically representing the Divine Word of God (the root meaning of the 'deus' means 'the shining one'). The angel Gabriel tells Mary She is to bring forth the Son of God. She replies, 'How can this be, seeing I know not a man?' (*Gospel of St Luke*). As soon as Mary accepts, She conceives Christ in Her womb. It is verily the moment when the Word becomes Flesh.

The passage in the *Bible* runs thus:

> Now in the sixth month, the archangel Gabriel was sent from God to a city of Galilee, named Nazareth, to a virgin pledged to be married to a man whose name was Joseph, of the house of David. The virgin's name was Mary. Having come in, the angel said to her, "Rejoice, you highly favored one! The Lord is with you. Blessed are you among women!" But when she saw him, she was greatly troubled at the saying, and considered what kind of salutation this might be. The angel said to her, "Don't be afraid, Mary, for you have found favor with God. Behold, you will conceive in your womb, and bring forth a son, and will call his name 'Jesus.' He will be great, and will be called the Son of the Most High. The Lord God will give him the throne of his father, David, and he will reign over the house of Jacob forever. There will be no end to his Kingdom." Mary said to the angel, "How can this be, seeing I am a virgin?" The angel answered her, "The Holy Spirit will come on you, and the power of the Most High will overshadow you. Therefore also the holy one who is born from you will be called the Son of God. Behold, Elizabeth, your relative, also has conceived a son in her old age; and this is the sixth month with her who was called barren. For everything spoken by God is possible." Mary said, "Behold, the handmaid of the Lord; be it to me according to your word." The angel departed from her.

There are different types of Annunciation images, depicting different moments in the apostles' story. The most challenging task for the painter is to portray the complex web of emotions in the Annunciation: the simultaneous fear and wonder, doubt and passion of the Virgin Mary.

The splendour of the Archangel Gabriel is relatively easy to describe: a peacock's feathers do well for him. For the Madonna, something more is required, something delicate and poignant. For Mary is required to express joy on one hand, but, as in all Christian religion, there must be humility too.

Fra Roberto Caracciolo organized the Annunciation into fifteen stages, grouped together in fives under three principal mysteries: the Angelic Mission, the Angelic Salutation, and the Angelic Colloquy.[2] It's in the Colloquy stage where the real drama of the Annunciation occurs, where there is a small amount of dialogue and negotiation. The fives stages are:

1. *Conturbio* (Disquiet)
2. *Cogitatio* (Reflection
3. *Interrogatio* (Inquiry)
4. *Humiliatio* (Submission)
5. *Meritatio* (Merit)

Most Renaissance *Annunciations* are of the Disquiet or Submission type. The versions of Sandro Botticelli, Fra Filippo Lippi, Leonardo da Vinci and Fra Angelico are clearly of the submissive kind, where the Virgin Mary psychologically prostrates Herself before the Lord, stating that She is His servant. Fra Roberto describes this moment of ritual humiliation thus:

> Lowering her head she spoke: *Behold the handmaid of the Lord.* She did not say 'Lady'; she did not say 'Queen'. Oh profound humility! oh extraordinary gentleness! 'Behold,' she said, 'the slave and servant of my Lord.'[3]

For some feminists, the Annunciation scenario is another example of Western patriarchy in action: a woman taken spiritually by force. For feminists, Mary is too passive, too humble, too acquiescent in Her fate. In the Annunciation, Mary is taken by force, without being able to refuse. Fra Angelico, though, does not question the patriarchal, traditional nature of the Annunciation (one would not expect a painter like Angelico to do so). For him, it is a quiet, mystical, humble moment, which he lovingly, meticulously paints. Looked at in the light of post-1970s radical feminism, Angelico's *Annunciations* seem sad, even pathetic. Yet they are also sweetly painted objects, the Virgin's 'passivity' in fact contains an inner strength. The German poet Rainer Maria Rilke (1875-1926) wrote a sequence of Madonna poems, his *Marien leben*, or *The Life of the Virgin Mary*, which express that sense of devotion and purity that Angelico was striving for:

> Nun soll ein neues sein,
> von dem der Erdkreis ringender sich weitet.
> Wast ist ein Dörnicht uns: Gott fühlt sich ein
> in einer Jungfrau Schooss. Ich bin der Schein
> von ihrer Innigkeit, der euch geleitet.

[Now shall a new thing be, by which the world shall spread in inter circles. What is a thornbush to us: God feels his way into a virgin's womb. I am the shine of her lovingness, that goes with you.]⁴

❧

Fra Angelico's early *Annunciation* in the *Cortona Altarpiece* of c. 1433 is a rich essay in gold, red and blue. These three colours obsessed Angelico, and recur throughout his career. In the *Cortona Annunciation* they are particularly emphatic: the colour red, for example, is deep and sonorous, appearing in the Virgin Mary's dress, the angel's costume, and the drape that protects the Madonna's chamber. Gold is strident here too: it appears in the braid edging of the Virgin's blue cloak, in the cloth of honour behind Her, in the Archangel's wings, and all over his costume.

The Archangel Gabriel is a mass of gestures and signs, commands which the Virgin Mary must obey. Rushing into the *loggia*, he gesticulates with his fingers, pointing upwards to indicate his origin and mission from God, and at the Madonna. As he points, three lines of words issue from his mouth, aimed at the Virgin's mouth, breast and halo. Above Her, in the shadows of the starry ceiling of the *loggia*, the dove hovers, golden flames erupting from its white body. The dove has a tiny halo on its head.

As the Annunciation traditionally occurred on March 25th, in Spring, the ground surrounding the *loggia* is starred with flowers in the *Cortona Altarpiece*. These flowers relate the Madonna to the mythic Goddess of

Flowers of ancient times, to notions of Mother Earth, that 'feminine' *participation mystique* with the Earth. The Annunciation scene thus depicts the human Mary becoming a Goddess. It shows Her entry into the full Christian story. Before this moment, Mary has been human: now is She more-than-human, yet still also human. Like Christ, She suffers a human life, and a human death. But She is marked out from the rest of humanity, for later She is welcomed bodily into Heaven. The Annunciation depicts the birth of a Goddess, or the annointing of a Goddess, or the coming of age of a Goddess. After the Annunciation, Mary's divinity is unquestionable. For if She bears the Son of God (who is also God), She must be divine Herself. In fact, the sense of holiness works back through Mary to Her mother, St Anne.

Christopher Lloyd writes thus of the Cortona *Annunciation* in his 1979 study of Fra Angelico:

> The main incident is bathed in the full glare of this light, which strikes the arches extending backwards in the picture with a similar force. Yet the Expulsion of Adam and Eve is shown with a supernatural light shining from the Garden of Paradise, 'fierce as a comet' in Milton's phrase. It is as though the Angel had suddenly opened a door, thereby emitting bright rays into the surrounding darkness. (8)

The Virgin Mary is the Second Eve. Fra Angelico points this out in many of his *Annunciations*. On the left, typically, we see Adam and Eve being expelled from Heaven by St Michael, brandishing a sword, the most terrible, fateful moment in Western religion, with the Crucifixion. Angelico's *Annunciations*, then, like other Renaissance *Annunciations*, depict the very moment of the Fall and its redemption by the coming of Christ. The expulsion of Adam and Eve is usually portrayed as a horrific, tragic event, with Adam and Eve weeping and holding their heads in grief (as in Masaccio's Brancacci Chapel fresco, 1427/28). The Annunciation rights the wrongs of the Fall, yet it is always depicted as a solemn, serious event. Never is the Annunciation shown as a wholly joyous experience, yet it should be, for everyone on Earth is redeemed by the imminent arrival of Christ. But no, Renaissance *Annunciations* are sombre affairs, with not even a slight smile being allowed.

✹

Fra Angelico's later *Annunciations* are more accomplished than the Cortona *Annunciation,* and much more spiritually intense. Angelico kept refining the Annunciation scene until he reached the simplicity and high emotion of *The Annunciation* (*c.* 1440) in the North dormitory corridor and in cell three at San Marco. In the latter fresco, the Archangel stands while Mary bows, Her arms crossed on Her breast. Mary here is so thin as to be nearly insubstantial: Her body is very much the Christian vessel waiting to be filled, the woman as pubescent virgin, distinctly pre-sexual and chaste.

The cell three *Annunciation* (1440-41) depicts a whitewashed space which mirrors the very cell and cloisters in which the painting is situated. Always Fra Angelico stresses the continuity between spiritual and earthly space, between the sacred, timeless world of the Christian story, and the secular, everyday world of the convent.

The pale, open lighting and space of the San Marco frescoes reduces the components of the paintings to simple but eloquent shapes. Nothing is allowed to intervene between spectator and subject matter. The reductive compositions and the light palette make the angel stand out when he appears. The Archangel's red gown, bright gold halo and fabulous peacock wings mark him out immediately as an extraordinary presence in the relatively everyday monastic cell. The high-toned cell is swept clean of all distractions. Only Peter Martyr on the left distracts momentarily from the central religious drama occurring between Gabriel and Mary. The Angel looks down on Mary kindly, not smiling, not wholly serious either. The Madonna stares past him, as so often in Angelico's paintings, into the distance, musing on Her future life. The Annunciation is an event which utterly alters the Virgin Mary's life, yet Angelico's versions of the event show the Madonna sitting very still, very quiet. 'As a statement about awe and tenderness, expressed in the simplest possible terms, Fra Angelico's painting has very few rivals', commented Edward Mullins in *The Painted Witch: Female Body, Male Art* (26)

Of course, even as we stress the simplicity and purity of Fra Angelico's paintings, which is so obvious in San Marco frescoes, we must also remember that all painting is a fiction, all painting is constructed, all painting comes out of a series of decisions – not only what to do, but also what *not* to do. While the painter may be concerned about using this or that paintbrush, or this or that colour, there are all manner of other factors coming into play, many of them unconsciously, for the artist. The 'simplicity' of Angelico's work, then, which contributes so much to his mysticism, is also a fiction and an illusion.

Perhaps the most poignant of Fra Angelico's *Annunciations* is the San Marco fresco in the North dormitory of about 1440. This *Annunciation* is painted in much deeper tones than the high-toned cell three *Annunciation*, with Angelico's usual range of colours. Here, the passivity of the Madonna is monumental. There is no figure so still and silent and calm and humble in all of Renaissance painting. Her cheeks blush softly; Her body leans forward gently; the angel mimics Her posture. The two of them seemed locked in a timeless ritual, the outer stillness masking the inner battle of wills. The Archangel Gabriel is gently teasing, ironic, confident of the outcome. The Virgin Mary is utterly immobile. Her static, silent stance suggests the weight of patriarchal authority and religious meaning which God is pressing down upon Her. The drama is played out in a disarmingly delicate way. Angelico's lyricism lifts it into the realms of greatness. He chooses his moment, and fixes it in time. Not a snapshot, but the compression of a religious revelation.

The North dormitory *Annunciation* is perhaps Fra Angelico's most oft-reproduced image in all his art. There is much to enjoy here: the flatness and detail of the little field with its red and white flowers; the wood behind the fence; the magnificence of the peacock wings of the Archangel; the subtle modelling of the Virgin Mary's face; the softness of Her blushing cheeks. One approaches it up a flight of stairs – it looms in front of the ascending viewer. It is a powerful devotional image, which commands a religious, ritualistic response from the onlooker. Along the bottom of the painting, for example, are the words:

VIRGINIS INTACTE CVM VENERIS ANTE FIGVRAM PRETEREVNDO CAVE NE SILEATVR AVE: *When you come before the image of the Ever-Virgin take care that you do not neglect to say an 'Ave'.*

There are intriguing aspects to the painting which one does not notice on first glance. The figures, for example, are huge, compared to the scale of the arcades; the Archangel does not cast a shadow, but the Virgin does; the vaulting in the fictional building does not fit in with the arcades; some of the capitals on the pillars are composite Ionic, while others are Corinthian. These inconsistencies pale into insignificance, however, when one considers the emotional power of the two figures, how they perpetually confront each other, how the eye flicks from one face to the other, as if in a call and response scenario, as if one can actually hear the words of the Archangel and the Madonna: his forceful but tender message, Her anxious, whispered reply.

There is the same harmony of delicacy, gentle line, suppressed spiritual emotion and theological pressure in another celebrated Renaissance *Annunciation*, Simone Martini's 1333 painting in the Uffizi Museum. Against a luminous golden ground, the Virgin Mary is connected to the Archangel Gabriel via a stream of holy words. The text literally spins from mouth to mouth, from the Angel's mouth to the Madonna's mouth. Significantly, it seems to be the words which seed the Virgin, demonstrating the all-pervading power of the Word in Christianity. In Martini's *Annunciation*, we see the Word becoming Flesh. Even if Martini hadn't painted those words flying from body to body, we know that the Word or speech can generate life in Western religion. For, it is at the very moment when God/ Gabriel speaks that the Virgin Mary becomes pregnant. God's speech or words is the vehicle for His seed. Faced with this forceful, phallic emissary of God, it is no wonder that the Madonna draws back from the stream of words in Simone Martini's painting. In a late 4th century Gnostic text, the *Epistula Apostolorum*, the events of the Annunciation are narrated from God's point of view;

> On that day when I took the form of the Angel Gabriel, I appeared to Mary and spoke with her. Her heart received me; She believed and laughed. And I, the Word, formed myself and entered into her womb; I became flesh; and I myself was servant for myself, and in the form of an angel...5

For painters as for theologians the Annunciation created more than a few problems. In this Gnostic text we see God becoming a shaman shape-changer: first he's angel, then a word, then a spermatozoon, then a foetus. Fra Angelico sticks to the central doctrinal tenets of the Annunciation, and depicts the moment in individual, personal terms, concentrating on the 'human' aspects of the scene: the meeting of two divine but actually flesh and blood figures. Angelico reduces the scene where the young Virgin imbibes the Holy Word and seed of God to its essentials. The tumultuous but static scene of the Annunciation becomes a drama of suppressed feelings and ascetic self-control.

In the Madrid *Annunciation* (late 1440s), the coaxing Archangel again emulates the Virgin's pose by crossing his arms over his chest. Yet Mary's gesture here seems as much one of defence as of humility, as if She is trying to prevent the Word-seed of God entering Her virginal body. She has foreseen the end of the whole Christian drama, and does not want a part in it.

Fra Angelico's usual pictorial geometry is symmetrical, or pyramidal. A similar emotional interplay occurs in the San Giovanni Val d'Arno *Annunciation* (1431), where the Virgin and the Archangel echo each other. This is one of Angelico's crudest *Annunciations*, in which the space and colour is awkward. In the Prado, Madrid *Annunciation* (1430-32), the Archangel Gabriel wears clothes in his flamboyant manner opposing those of the Virgin Mary: his opulent red clothes fall open at the ankle to reveal the coldness of divinity beneath. In the same way, Mary's cool blue outer robe falls aside to reveal the crimson dress, symbolizing Her livingness. The painting depicts the meeting of an abstract masculine sky-god with an earthbound feminine presence. It shows a woman in the process of becoming a Goddess, with all the problems that entails.

Fra Angelico's *Annunciations* depict the eternally paradoxical drama of religion. They show the meeting in the same space of the sacred and the earthly, the supernatural and the worldly. They show the appropriation and incorporation of the Wholly Other into a human scheme. Angelico's *Annunciations* re-ritualize a moment already ritualized *ad infinitum* in Christianity up to the Quattrocento.

✳

The emotional content of Fra Angelico's paintings is generally a cosmic melancholy. His figures – his Madonnas especially – are very sad. Rarely does a smile appear on anyone's face. His Madonnas are wistful, always looking down, or into the distance, seldom looking at the viewer, or anything in particular in the painting. It is the same with Fra Filippo Lippi's Madonnas, or those of Sandro Botticelli or Titian or Quentin Massys. Leonardo da Vinci, it seems, is rare among Renaissance painters in giving the Madonna his famous Gioconda Smile. Angelico's Madonnas hold Their child, seemingly in the 'bloom of motherhood', to use a typical cliché, but always looking down, head titled, eyes open but staring, unfocused, into nothing, mouth fixed straight, or, often turning down slightly. Julia Kristeva writes in "Motherhood According to Bellini":

> The face of [Bellini's] Madonnas are turned away, intent on something
> else that draws their gaze to the side, up above, or nowhere in
> particular, but never centres it in the baby. (1986, 247)

There is not much laughter, humour or even joy in Christianity. Instead of emphasizing the Resurrection of Christ, that joyous bursting back into life after the Crucifixion, it is significant that painters concentrate on the Pietà or the Crucifixion, the dead Christ, looking pathetic and mournful as he is dragged from the Cross and laid in the tomb. This woeful glorific-ation of suffering is at the heart of the Christian religion. This sad feeling of the Pietà and Crucifixion paintings also suffuses the Madonna and Child paintings.

One feels like asking the Blessed Virgin Mary: why are you so sad? The answer is that She is a masculine creation, the image of male projections, about patriarchal attitudes towards women and motherhood. In Christ-ianity, it seems you can't be seen to smile or laugh when 'great', 'important' emotions are being portrayed. You can't smile *and* be serious about motherhood; you can't laugh as you ponder death. There are no smiles at the Crucifixion, even though we all know the Son of God ascends after his 'human' death. Similarly, the Madonna is not shown smiling, except in rare cases.

IV

The Madonna In the Renaissance

IT IS USEFUL to remind ourselves of the social, ideological and religious atmosphere of the Renaissance epoch. Although Fra Giovanni Beato Angelico da Fiesole is thought of primarily as a painter of glorious *Madonna and Child* images, the *Crucifixion* was the main religious image of the Renaissance. All of the major (and many of the minor) Renaissance painters made *Crucifixions* as well as *Madonna and Child* paintings (Angelico painted many *Crucifixions* at San Marco). Famous Renaissance *Crucifixions* include those by Rogier van der Weyden, Andrea Mantegna, Diego Velásquez, Masaccio and Raphael Sanzio. One aspect of Christian and Renaissance imagery that most Christian thinkers did not acknowledge was the eroticism of the Saviour's naked body. Everyone else in the Crucifixion drama is clothed, but Christ is nearly nude. If we accept that *any* nude has an erotic component, as more commentators than Kenneth Clark have noted, then the eroticism of Christ's naked body must be addressed. Few art critics have acknowledged the eroticism of the naked Christ, yet it is certainly a significant element in the great depictions of Christ on the Cross: by Peter Rubens, Velásquez and Mantegna. Christ's nakedness sends out conflicting signals. Clearly, nudity has a religious or mythic aspect, connoting nature/naturalness, purity, birth, creation, re-nunciation, unveiled reality and truth. In art, however, nudity is ambiguous: in religious contexts it is both spiritual and sexual, a duality which painters often exploited. Christ's body in Renaissance painting is often sexless, or androgynous, or feminized. Christianity is an ambivalent cult; it has a clothed, virginal woman as the object of worship on the one hand, and a naked, equally virginal and chaste man on the other. In the most holy of churches, nudity is sanctified by the statues, icons and paintings of Christ on the Cross.

The dying or dead Christ, naked but for a slip of cloth and sometimes depicted entirely naked but with His legs bent to one side, hiding the 'transcendent signifier', the phallus, is also an image of homoeroticism. Theologians and art historians down the ages did not or would not admit that Christ was or could have been an object of lust. Yet this is clearly the case in some depictions of the naked Saviour, such as paintings by Giovanni Battista Rosso, Michelangelo Merisi da Caravaggio, or Antonello da Messina. These nude figures send out a mass of signals, from the pathetic to the narcissistic, from the erotic to the spiritual.

Yet, somehow, Fra Angelico's work seems to sidestep the discourses of sexuality, notions of gender and sexual identity. Angelico's figures do not seem concerned with sexuality or gender at all, and Angelico's Christ is one of the most chaste and un-sexual in all Western art. While Raphael's or Michelangelo Buonaroti's near-nude Saviours openly display their bodies in an erotic fashion, Angelico's Christs are not interested in such exhibitionism. Instead, Angelico's Christ figures, like those in Early Netherlandish painting (Rogier van der Weyden, Gerard David, Petrus Christus), deflect the sexual connotations and urge the viewer to consider the pathos and suffering of the Crucifixion.

Throughout Renaissance painting, the Mother seems to be primary: the central image is the Mother nursing Her Child. At the Crucifixion, the Mother is present, witnessing Her son's death. Sometimes the 'three Marys' are depicted. But the Madonna is present in another way: She is the wooden Cross upon which he writhes in agony. The Madonna has always been central to Renaissance religious painting: She is not only central to Renaissance religious painting, She is at the visual centre of most Renaissance paintings. She is the focus of the paintings. She sits on a throne, or stands, and is at the centre.

It is the same with depictions of the Crucifixion: the Cross is central, and the Cross is the Mother, symbolically (as well as symbolizing other things). Jesus sits on his Mother's lap, just as Horus sits on the lap of the Egyptian Goddess Isis. At his death, too, Jesus rests on the body of his Mother. This mystery – of the present/ absent Mother – is found throughout Renaissance art.

Renaissance Madonna art reveals the ambiguous relationship societies have with their mothers, with their bodies, in a love/ hate, presence/ absence conflict. Julia Kristeva has written eloquently of the relation between the maternal, gender, identity and desire in Renaissance art (in "Motherhood According to Bellini"):

> ...craftsmen of Western art reveal better than anyone else the artist's debt to the maternal body and/or motherhood's entry into symbolic existence – that is, translibidinal *jouissance*, eroticism taken over by the language of art. Not only is a considerable portion of pictorial art devoted to motherhood, but within this representation itself, from Byzantine iconography to Renaissance humanism and the worship of the body that it initiates, two attitudes toward the maternal body emerge, prefiguring two destinies within the very economy of Western representation. Leonardo Da Vinci and Giovanni Bellini seem to exemplify in the best fashion the opposition between these two attitudes. On the one hand, there is a tilting toward the body as fetish. On the other, a predominance of luminous, chromatic differences beyond and despite corporeal representation. Florence and Venice. Worship of the figurable, representable man; or integration of the image accomplished in its truthlikeness within the luminous serenity of the unrepresentable.[1]

Although She is at the heart of Renaissance painting, the Madonna is decentred, psychologically and theologically. Although She is the Mother of God, his geneatrix, his womb, his birth, She is decentred, sidelined, displaced. The treatment of the Virgin Mary is complex in Renaissance painting and in Western religion. She is eroticized, for a start: most, if not all, Renaissance Madonna and Child paintings eroticize the Madonna. Yet, at the same time, She is desexualized; the actualities of motherhood are smoothed over. Breast feeding is shown, but the attitude to it is ambivalent, as it is still is today, where people get uptight when they see someone breast feeding in public.[2]

Against science, in the Renaissance era, there is religion. The Madonna presides over the religious domain. Julia Kristeva writes:

> There is Christian theology (especially canonical theology); but theology defines maternity only as an impossible elsewhere, a sacred beyond, a vessel of divinity, a spiritual tie with the virginal and committed to assumption. (in ib., 237)

Indeed, to be so slavishly worshipped, as the Madonna is throughout Her history and throughout the Catholic world, from Sao Paolo to St Petersburg, is not simply positive and enriching. It puts Her in a particular position which, understandably, She was probably reluctant to accept. You see this reluctance in the Renaissance paintings of the Annunciation. As Andrea Dworkin writes in her book *Right-Wing Women*, it is not always honey and milk to be worshipped as a Goddess:

> To stay worshipped, the woman must stay a symbol and she must stay good. She cannot become merely a human in the muck of life, morally flawed and morally struggling, committing acts that have complex, difficult, unpredictable consequences. ...The worshipping attitude, the spiritual elevation of women that men invoke whenever they suggest that women are finer than they, proposes that women are what men can never be: chaste, good. In fact men are what women can never be: real moral agents, the bearers of real moral authority and responsibility.[3]

Andrea Dworkin's ruthless polemic is simplistic: it polarizes notions of masculine and feminine and rides over ambiguities, yet when we apply it to the Virgin Mary, how accurate it seems, in its basic thrust.

French feminist Julia Kristeva's "Motherhood According to Bellini" is a brilliant analysis of not only Giovanni Bellini, but also many other Renaissance painters. What Kristeva has to say about Bellini also applies to Fra Angelico, Sandro Botticelli, Leonardo da Vinci, Piero della

Francesca, Andrea Mantegna, Giotto and others. Kristeva discusses the portrayal of the maternal body in the Renaissance painter's art. In Kristeva's reading of Renaissance philosophy, the woman is simultaneously allowed to be and not to be the mother; She is placed centrally and simultaneously decentred; She is exalted by painters even as She is denigrated. Kristeva comments:

> The language of art, too, follows (but differently and more closely) the other aspect of maternal *jouissance*, the sublimation taking place at the very moment of primal repression within the mother's body, arising perhaps unwittingly out of her marginal position. At the intersection of sign and rhythm, of representation and light, of the symbolic and the semiotic, the artist speaks from a place where she is not, where she knows not. (ib, 242)

Present in the painting, the real woman is elsewhere. This is clear when we look at Renaissance Madonnas: the 'real' woman, the flesh and blood, living and breathing woman is elsewhere. She is not in the painting. The painted Madonna is a cipher, a symbol, 'pure figment', as Samuel Beckett says of his Goddess figure in *Ill Seen, Ill Said*. Life is elsewhere said the guru of the Surrealists, André Breton, and in Renaissance paintings, the actual mother is elsewhere. Geoffrey Ashe in his book *The Virgin* calls Mary 'the obscure Jewish wife', remarking that it is amazing that this 'obscure Jewish wife' should become one of the central figures of Western culture, subject of thousands of Renaissance paintings, not to mention mediæval cathedral sculpture.

Any religious painting is an interface between the human and the divine, between the secular and the sacred. It is an uneasy, ambiguous relationship. The painting is both a mundane object, a bit of wood, canvas and pigment, purchased in the dusty streets in a town, brought back to the studio, and put together by the painter (and assistants). The painting-as-object is thoroughly secular, thoroughly ordinary. Yet it is also a sacred object, a piece of magic. The painter works with solid, real materials to create something that is illusion, not very solid, really; the painting is something unreal, insubstantial, ethereal, impossible to grasp, something powerful though; in short, something magical.

Painters of all eras wrestle with these physical, semantic, psychological, æsthetic and metaphysical tensions. The tensions between abstraction and representation, between 'illusion' and 'reality', between colour and 'life'. The religious painter has to deal with the ever-impossible task: the depiction of the invisible and the unknown. The artist has to make the ungraspable graspable, as Julia Kristeva notes in *Desire in Language*:

> The artist, as servant of the maternal phallus, displays this always and everywhere unaccomplished art of reproducing bodies and spaces as graspable, masterable objects, within reach of his eye and hand. (246)

Renaissance Madonnas present a *jouissance* of maternal space that is, Julia Kristeva writes, 'beyond discourse, beyond narrative, beyond psychology, beyond lived experience and biography' (ib., 247).

Renaissance Madonnas are eroticized through selective parts of the body. Her body is always clothed: the idea of a nude Virgin Mary is blasphemous. We do not see the Virgin naked, ever. We see, in fact, only Her face and hands, sometimes Her neck. Her body is always covered up. And not just loosely covered, but thickly, heavily covered, heaped up with blue and crimson robes, dresses, wimples and hoods. (Sometimes She offers Her breast to the child).

Fra Angelico learnt, like every Renaissance painter, how to make folds in clothes expressive. Angelico's are not the deep, shadowy folds of Leonardo da Vinci or Perugino, but they are 'the luminous folds and secret depths of the sacred', as Julia Kristeva calls them (260). These folds are themselves part of the overall eroticization of the Virgin, and of motherhood. Unable to paint the body of the Mother of God, Renaissance painters threw themselves into painting Her face and hands, and Her clothes. The Madonna's wardrobe is always rich, always indicative of profusion and luxury. The Blessed Virgin Mary is the mother the painter always wanted: quiet, subdued, passive, nurturing, enfolding the child in swathes of love and connection, symbolized by the arms and hands around the child, and those luxuriant robes.

The folds in the Virgin's mantle are a way of painting the power of the Virgin without revealing Her body, the body which has to be absent, as

Julia Kristeva points out:

> The image of the Virgin – the woman whose entire body is an emptiness
> through which the paternal word is conveyed – had remarkably sub-
> sumed the maternal "abject," which is so necessarily intrapsychic.[4]

Not 'feminist', then, Renaissance paintings of the Madonna uphold
every stereotype of 'woman' and 'motherhood' you care to imagine. It
could not be otherwise, considering the socio-political context, the desires
of the patrons, and the æsthetic and Christian conventions which had been
centuries in the making. In fact, Fra Angelico does not question stereotypes
at all: he maintains them. He depicts the Madonna as the drudge of
humanity, the drudge as Goddess. Angelico's Madonna, like all Renaissance Madonnas, is really a mask, of something that remains always out-
of-reach. The Madonna, as Julia Kristeva notes, 'increasingly appears as a
module, a process' (ib., 264).

> Nowhere else but here, it seems, in the luminous folds and secret depths
> of the sacred that painting strives to capture; with regard to it, the myth
> of the maternal figure is nothing but a screen, a foreground, or an
> obstruction to be broken through. (in ib., 260)

Joseph Campbell speaks of the 'masks of God', and Fra Angelico's
paintings are like Russian icons, objects that point beyond themselves, to
some mystery beyond. The 'mystery beyond' is that Other, the primal
mother, the space Angelico (and no artist) can ever fully grasp.

V

Fra Angelico's Virgin Mary

AT FIRST GLANCE, Fra Giovanni Beato Angelico da Fiesole's Madonnas seem to be all sweetness, shyness and passivity. Their acquiescence seems to be monumental. In Her eyes, though, we begin to perceive the tragedy and pain beneath the beautiful exterior form. In the *Linaiuoli Altarpiece* (1433), for instance, the Madonna seems to be thinking not of Her Child, but of Her fate. The Child stands on Her knee, staring at the spectator and gesturing hieratically. The Virgin Mary, however, looks past the Child's halo into the distance, as so often in Angelico's paintings. She sinks into a thoughtful reverie. The soft tempera colours of the *Linaiuoli Altarpiece* encourage this pensive, melancholy atmosphere. Opulent gold drapes part to reveal the niche in which the Virgin sits, enthroned. Her hands gently support the Child. Her cheek is softly blushing.

One of the typical aspects of Fra Angelico's Madonnas is the gentility of their gestures. They tilt their heads to one side (usually Her left), looking down slightly. Angelico created these soft, thoughtful Madonnas through-out his career: in the *Annalena Altarpiece* (1437-40), in the sensuous *Bosco ai Frati Altarpiece* (c. 1450), and in the Bergamo *Madonna of Humility with Child and Angels* (1450-55, Galleria Dell'Accademia Carrara, Bergamo). As always with Renaissance Madonnas (such as Stefan Lochner's exquisite *Madonna in a Rose Garden* [1450, Cologne] or Fra Filippo Lippi's *Barbadori Altarpiece* [1437]), Angelico's Virgins exude a stillness and quietness which modulates the opulent settings. As with Leonardo da Vinci's astonishing *The Adoration of the Magi* (1480, Uffizi), the Madonna is the still centre of the religious drama. She supports the meanings and the web of relationships in the Renaissance painting. In Renaissance art, the Madonna sits at the centre. Around pivot all the other figures, the saints, donors and angels. Even the Child sits to one side of the Virgin Mary who stands or sits at the geometric, visual (and symbolic) centre. Without the Madonna there at the centre of the painting, the religious drama falls apart. The mythic Mother is essential. Angelico's Madonna paintings, like those of Lippi, Stefan Lochner, Piero della Francesca, Quentin Massys, Raphael Sanzio, Masaccio, Duccio di Buoninsegna, Simone Martini and Sandro Botticelli, demonstrate this unequivocally. She may be still and quiet and passive, but the Virgin Mary is also the foundation and spiritual centre of the paintings.

The *San Marco Altarpiece* (*The Virgin and Child Enthroned with Angels and Saints Cosmas and Damian, Lawrence, John the Evangelist, Mark, Dominic, Francis, and Peter Martyr*, 1438-40) is one of Fra Angelico's populous panels, roughly two yards square. The background comprise lines of dark fir, cypress, orange, pomegranate and palm trees. Just discernible beyond the trees is the sea – a rarity in *Madonna and Child* paintings. It is a pungent evocation of nature that Fra Angelico paints: the grass, trees, sky and sea are Angelico's most exquisite. Above the throng there are garlands of flowers. There is a feeling of festivity about the painting, even though, as expected, no one smiles, and the Virgin Mary looks particularly woeful.

The composition of the *San Marco Altarpiece* is pyramidal, a richly woven Oriental carpet anchors the structure with its powerful sense of perspective. Behind the throne is a brocaded drape, which separates the divine spectacle in the foreground from nature beyond. There is an open space in front of the Virgin, the kind of space that invites the spectator to step into the painting. Angelico emphasizes the theatricality of the scene by including golden drapes that hang each side. These theatrical motifs were dropped in the San Marco frescoes, making them all the more powerful.

The *San Marco Altarpiece* by Fra Angelico hovers between illusion and 'realism', between frontality and depth, between symbolism and naturalism. Sadly, as with the Bergamo *Madonna of Humility with Child and Angels*, the paint surface of the *San Marco Altarpiece* is somewhat deteriorated. The panel has lost its frame, and I quite like that. Purists of the Renaissance period might prefer to see everything of the era framed as it was meant to look. Sometimes, though, the lack of a frame helps to appreciate different aspects of the painting.

The *San Domenico Altarpiece* (1430s, Cortona) was modernized by Lorenzo de Credi around 1500. The gold background was turned into a landscape. The sweetness of the central Madonna is heightened by the very pale and greenish tinge to the skin, though it is not as green as the skin in the *Annalena Altarpiece* (1437-40, San Marco). An early work, the *San Domenico Altarpiece* is not one of Fra Angelico's more successful paintings, although the *predella* contains a vast panoply of gathered saints and angels celebrating a victorious Christ (one of the few Angelicos in the National Gallery, London).

The *Annalena Altarpiece* (1437-38) is one of Fra Angelico's less successful excursions. It has not been improved, either, by restoration. The colouration in the *Annalena Altarpiece* leaves much to be desired: the light green of the arcade behind the cloth of honour is an odd choice, while the cloth of honour itself is crudely gilded.

The *San Pier Martire Altarpiece* (1429), in San Marco, is another pseudo-*sacra conversazione* composition, again with the light greenish hue to the skin of the Madonna and Child. Gold predominates here, over three panels which depict a unified space. The size of the Madonna, as in other Fra Angelico altarpieces, is monumental: She might be about ten feet tall if She stood up, if you relate Her scale to the four saints who stand on each side. While not as impressive as a whole as some of Fra Angelico's later Madonnas, the *San Pier Martire Altarpiece* does contains some beautiful details, such as the golden cloth of honour that hangs behind the Virgin.

The *Cortona Altarpiece* (c. 1433) presents a discontinuous space over a triptych format, with the throne set back from the frontal plane. The awkwardness of the design suggests that Fra Angelico changed his plans during the course of painting it. The Madonna in the *Cortona Polyptych* recalls the Madonna of the *San Marco Triptych*. The Virgin's hand is placed gently on Her breast, holding Her cloak together. It is a gesture that suggests humility, the kind of gesture people make when bowing – one arm is folded back into the body, the other spread outwards. The gesture appears also in the East dormitory painting *Madonna and Child with Eight Saints*.

In this latter painting, sometimes known as *The Madonna of the Shadows*, Fra Angelico's delight in detail is apparent: in amongst the large blocks of colour, there are small passages of finely detailed painting, as in the little gold star that appears on the Virgin's blue cloak, on Her right shoulder, or the capitals on the four pilasters. The shadows of the title refer to the shadows on the white back wall, a bright, revealing light, quite different from the soft luminescence of the creamy-coloured frescoes (such as in *The Presentation in the Temple*, *The Coronation of the Virgin* and *The Transfiguration*).

But while the illumination and the clarity of the architectonics in *The Madonna of the Shadows* is æsthetically pleasing, guaranteed to excite a response from a budding John Ruskin or Walter Pater, it is the Christ child that is most arresting about the painting. He stares directly and forcibly at the spectator (as do the Saints Lawrence and Dominic). Jesus lifts his hand in blessing. He sits face-on to the viewer. His demeanour recalls if nothing else the direct, self-possessed stare and posture of the resurrected Christ. The child in *The Madonna of the Shadows* sits on Mary's lap but looks as if he is standing, as in paintings of the Resurrection. He looks very much like a future Messiah, a future world leader. His self-confidence is palpable, and the luminosity of the rest of the painting backs this up.

The connections between Fra Angelico's *Transfiguration* and *The Madonna of the Shadows* are obvious: it's as if Christ knows full well his future programme on Earth, and is fully confident about carrying it out. The child in *The Madonna of the Shadows* stares into the future and sees that it is good. He knows what to do. The Madonna here supports and is secondary to the child: although She is centre frame, visually, it is Christ who dominates the painting. He has just been born; in the Resurrection he is born again: in the first instance, he comes out of the woman; the second from the 'feminine' womb of the Earth.

Fra Angelico's *Perugia Triptych* (1437-38) is the same format as the *Cortona Altarpiece*, but is more opulent. The sense of space is more unified, too, and the colours are more satisfying. The overriding impression is of gold, which saturates the interior of the painting as well as the elaborate frame. The heart of the *Perugia Polyptych* is one of Angelico's most wistful Madonnas. She is bulky, monumental, dressed in the typical Fra Angelico style, with the outer blue cloak braided with gold, held together by a golden brooch, the red dress underneath revealed as the Virgin moves to support the Child on Her lap. As so often in Fra Angelico's art, the red dress spills onto the floor: parts of it are visible underneath the cloak. Again, one notices little details which makes Angelico's painting so enriching: the hands, for example: the soft gesture of the Madonna, touching Her son's elbow; the hands of the angels behind the throne who rest them gently on the side of the throne; the hands of the saint holding his book, his fingers brushing the edges of the gilded pages.

The Turin *Madonna and Child* (1433) is one of Fra Angelico's sweetest. Cleverly, Angelico leaves the Virgin's face very soft. There are no signs of age or exhaustion on Her face. She is luminous and beautiful, as if seen through gauze. The Blessed Virgin's costume, meanwhile, is very detailed: the brooches, the jewels, the gold braid edging Her cloak are all painted with care. Angelico dexterously contrasts the hardness of objects such as the throne and walls in his paintings with the softness of flesh, especially faces and hands. Behind the Virgin's head is a large halo which looks like one of the round and ornate plates, the *tondo*, that were popular at the time in Florence.

The *Bosco ai Frati Altarpiece* (c. 1450) in San Marco depicts a single unified space with the Madonna enthroned at the centre, Her cloak spilling over towards the viewer and outwards to the gathering of the saints and bishops. The golden apse behind the Virgin Mary looks forward to many of Giovanni Bellini's altarpieces. The floor is decorated with those smudgy pastel shapes that Fra Angelico made his own, which are found in so much of his art, and which are essentially abstract. The *Bosco ai Frati Altarpiece* has the illusionistic depth and dark tonality of Fra Angelico's later paintings. As in the *San Marco Altarpiece,* there is a line of shadowy trees in the background, seen against a very dark sky. The architectonics of the *Bosco di Frati Altarpiece* are carefully worked out and successfully executed. The wall and apse are depicted with a convincing sense of illusion, even though Fra Angelico maintains a sense of unreality in his haloes, always seen flat and face-on to the viewer. At this stage, Fra Angelico is still somewhere between mediæval and Renaissance art: the archaic methods of signifying divinity persisted long after mediæval and Byzantine forms of depicting bodies and architecture had been surpassed by Renaissance perspective and space. Even in 'sophisticated' High Renaissance painting, such as in Raphael Sanzio's art, haloes still appear, giving the art an archaic, ritualistic appearance.

✳

In Fra Angelico's altarpieces (the *San Marco Altarpiece,* or the *San Domenico Altarpiece,* for example), the *sacra conversazione* is played out, as it is in all Renaissance *sacra conversazione,* in complete silence. These are 'sacred conversations' in which there is no conversation. No one says anything. No one looks at anyone else. Most Virgin Marys in *sacra conversazione* paintings look down, sad, mute (She is 'caught in the grips of primal repression', as Julia Kristeva puts it [1986, 262]). Saints such as Lucy and Catherine of Alexandria stand either side of the Madonna on the throne, also looking down; saints Peter Martyr, Francis, Lawrence and Jerome often flank them, looking down also, lost in thought.

The result is a silent interplay of contemplation; each figure muses in their own space, connected visually but not emotionally to the other figures. This is very apparent in many *sacra conversazione* paintings: the distance between one person and the next, despite their physical proximity. In many paintings of *The Virgin and Child With Saints,* as the *sacra conversazione* images are often titled, we find this melancholy meditation suffusing the picture: the evocations are of timelessness, as if these figures have been standing or sitting in those poses forever. Nothing moves, no flutter of wind, there is no sound, no crying of children outside the picture, no ill-mannered gestures, nothing uncouth or inappropriate.

The *sacra conversazione* paintings are remarkably silent, motionless paintings, where the paint is smoothed onto the wood panel or canvas without a single ripple, where no external forces disturb the inner calm of the protagonists; where no one shows any emotion other than quiet introspection. After all, the Child sitting on the Madonna's lap is a time for rejoicing, surely? The Child is young, the Madonna is young – it's a young mom and her new baby! – but these pictures have an incredible emotional weight about them: they are heavy images, full of the weight of death, of sadness, of fate.

The *sacra conversazione* paintings are an impossible situation: the divine appearing in person, on Earth, in a space at once sacred and secular. There sits the Virgin and Her child, and the mystery remains total to the end, because She is divine, yet She appears on Earth, that is, in a profane realm. These Renaissance paintings depict, then, the meeting of the impossible (divinity) with the possible (Earth). It is impossible that the Virgin is there at all; it is impossible that She is a virgin yet She has a child. Every Madonna and Child painting repeats this mystery. For, there She is, a virgin, but with Her own child on Her knee.

Fra Angelico paints these fusions of the sacred and the secular with a quiet confidence, emphasizing the solemnity and sacrality of the event, the painting of the costumes and faces of the saints and donors is never allowed to be too voluptuous, to distract from the spiritual import. Angelico's paintings rehearse the inrush of the sacred, but in the quietest, most thoughtful and circumspect manner.

Fra Angelico's paintings are not full of music, like, say, Piero della Francesca's marvellous and sonorous London *Nativity* (1470), where the five angels sing loudly. In Angelico's paintings, one imagines the scene to be very quiet. Set against the marble steps and green and red hangings, the costumes of the saints and noblemen and divinities in Angelico's pictures stand out brilliantly. All is tranquillity in Angelico's paintings. The figures tirelessly retain their symbolic poses, hands clasping books, swords, staffs and musical instruments. The austerity of the spiritual dimension is offset by the opulence of the costumes and settings.

✳

One of Fra Angelico's best works is undoubtedly the *Coronation of the Virgin* (1432, in the Louvre Museum, Paris). When you contemplate the painting in the flesh after seeing it in reproductions you are struck by the usual things you hadn't quite realized (the size and scale, the sensuous surface, the physicality of the painting, the frame, the lighting in the gallery, the relation to other works, etc). But what is stunning is the colouration, which is the richest Angelico created. The coronation takes place on a tall throne and platform which is profusely decorated with gold. Behind the throne is a brilliant blue sky, one of those timeless blue Florentine skies, the sort that decorate the ceilings in the palaces of Florence, and also the sort of sky that can still be seen in Tuscany in Spring and Summer especially. The colour highpoint of *The Coronation of the Virgin* in the Louvre is the long series of steps that lead up to Jesus and Mary. John White describes Angelico's *Coronation* thus, in *The Birth and Rebirth of Pictorial Space*:

> the patterned floor and the alignment of the inwards turning figures tell of the new distance to be travelled before reaching the now monumental flight of steps that leads to the high throne. The low viewpoint gives a stronger space, clearer support for the new weight of figures. On the other hand the colour underlines the interest in the overall surface pattern with which the climbing composition fills the panel. Going downwards on the left the colour runs from lilac to a pale pink, almost shell, and then on the right runs upwards from vermilion, through soft pinks, and back to lilac. But whilst this circling range of pinks harmonizes with the spatial content, without in any way expressing it in naturalistic terms, cooling, and softening as it recedes and climbs, it is everywhere associated with a bright pale blue. Unlike the pink, this endlessly repeated blue is quite unvaried from the figures in the foreground to the distant sky. It has no spatial function other than to unify the colour pattern with the flat pictorial surface. The separate roles of the two dominant elements in the colour are as clearly distinguished as the dual intention of the architectural construction. (171)

The Louvre *Coronation of the Virgin* is a truly majestic painting. Filled by a pale blue luminescence, the beloved azure of the Italian Renaissance, the *Coronation of the Virgin* is a direct, unapologetic celebration of Christ-

ianity. The range of colours is startling. One thinks of the Early Renaissance in terms of, primarily, gold, red and blue. Leonardo da Vinci spoke
of those painters who lived in the blue and the gold. In *The Coronation of
the Virgin*, though, Fra Angelico reminds us that the poetry of colour in the
Early Renaissance extends beyond a narrow range, and embraces violets
and pinks, soft greens and vermillions.

VI

Fra Angelico at San Marco, Florence

ITALY HAS MANY great crowd-pulling factors that draw tourists to it, among them food, climate, landscape and culture. On the culture trail, tourists flock to centres such as Venice, Rome, Naples, Siena, Pisa and Florence. The German poet Rainer Maria Rilke, like so many poets, went to Italy and found it overwhelmingly beautiful: in letters to his Muse, Lou Andreas-Salomé, Rilke spoke of the 'painted God in gold' skies of Florence, the wild roses along the white gravelled paths, the 'gentle Madonnas' in the galleries. Of Venice, Rilke said that being there was the 'golden dome' on the 'palace of heavenly treasures' of his holiday. The 'stone fairy tale' of Venice utterly enchanted him.[1] Rilke's response to Italy is typical of so many other writers and poets (Percy Bysshe Shelley, John Keats, Thomas Hardy, Lord Byron, Johann Wolfgang von Goethe and John Ruskin).

The most beautiful location in Florence, however, is not the Pitti Palace, nor the Uffizi Museum, nor Filippo Brunelleschi's dome, nor the River Arno, nor Michelangelo Buonarroti's Medici tombs or Library, but Fra Giovanni Beato Angelico da Fiesole's San Marco Museum. It really is the most exquisite place in an already overly-exquisite city. In the San Marco

Museum in Florence you find Renaissance glorification. Everywhere you look there is glory. It really is the highpoint of a Florentine stay.

The Convent of San Marco was rebuilt by the Medicis after 1437. Now the San Marco Museum, it is the place one *must* visit to discover the essence of Fra Beato Angelico da Fiesole's art. It is the primary place for an Angelico pilgrimage. For Leonardo da Vinci fans, the Louvre is high up on the lists of targets; for Vincent van Gogh lovers, there is Amsterdam and Arlès; for J.M.W. Turner followers, the Clore Gallery in London, and so on. To find such a concentration of one artist's works in one place is rare (there is the Gustav Moreau Museum in Paris, for instance, which is wonderful).

It's a pity other artists do not have such a concentration of their works as Fra Angelico has at the San Marco Museum. Downstairs there is a room full of major Angelico pieces. He comes across, because of this focussing of works in one building, as a much bigger artist than he might do if we saw single Angelico pieces alongside Masaccio, Fra Filippo Lippi and Sandro Botticelli. Intensity is necessary: intense concentration and contemplation. This is what the San Marco Museum provides, for it is not only a collection of Fra Angelico paintings, it was also a Dominican priory, a place of worship on its own.

The building is beautiful, and kept in good condition. The corridors are swept clean, and are sparsely furnished. There are no extraneous furnishings to detract from the experience of enjoying Fra Angelico's art. So often Italian museums are a mess, in one way or another. They're often expensive, dimly lit, badly signposted, there are no guidebooks or floorplans, pictures are hung next to the window (as as the Pitti Palace), or hung five high up the walls (again, at the Pitti Palace), or they have surly, unhelpful guards, or they're too full of tourists (don't try to view Michelangelo Buonarroti's Sistine Chapel in the Vatican during the Summer months). Italian museums can be frustrating, with their odd policies and terrible sense of organization. The San Marco Museum in Florence, however, is really extraordinary.

It has been carefully restored. The monk's cells are marvellous, not at all oppressive or cloyingly monastic or 'religious' in the traditional sense.

It is not dusty and fusty as so many churches are. The cells are simple, sparse, washed with a creamy white paint. The frescoes fit perfectly. They are softly matt, without a sheen. Only the blood gleams. Devoid of frames, of fancy attachments, of titles, of anything but themselves, they are all the more powerful. Seen together, all at once: overwhelming. Each cell contains a mystery. Each cell is made for a meditation on mystery. How soft and quiet it must have been before cars and machines.

The sequence of paintings and cells follows the story of the Passion, but roughly. *The Crucifixion* appears most often. The sequence is punctuated by a variety of *Crucifixions*. These are torturous – truly anguished.[2] Fra Angelico's art is seemingly so simple, yet capable of such spiritual heights. The same familiar Angelico faces appear.

It was a real breakthrough for Fra Angelico, on an æsthetic level, as a painter, to use white and a high-toned palette in some of the key paintings in the San Marco Museum. *The Transfiguration* (1439-43) and *The Coronation of the Virgin* – both in white – stand out. They surpass, in the depth of their spiritual feeling, even the *Descent From the Cross* (also in San Marco), and the Louvre *Coronation of the Virgin*.[3] The semi-circular top to each image fits so well into the hemi-spherical architecture of the cells. The light in these two paintings is dazzling. 'The light in the *Coronation* is entirely celestial,' as William Hood puts it in *Fra Angelico at San Marco* (233). C.G. Argan in *The Renaissance* associates Angelico's light with nature, with God's plan as revealed to humanity on Earth. 'Nature in her perfect state as created by God is only conceivable as being totally luminous' (22).

Fra Angelico employed both transparent and opaque layers of paint. The actors are robed in white, and are painted against a light background. Emphasizing the circular composition of *The Coronation of the Virgin* is a circular rainbow which surrounds the Mother of God and Her son. The rainbow gives the painting an apocalyptic edge, recalling the visions of the last book of the *Bible, Revelations* (Fra Filippo Lippi used the rainbow in one of his late frescoes). Mary and Jesus sit together, facing each other, their robes touching at their feet. The two figures echo each other at many points.

It's not difficult to see in the Coronation itself a moment when Mary and

Jesus face each other as something like equals. Indeed, Mother and Son are depicted in some Renaissance *Coronations* as lovers, or as would-be lovers, in a *unio mystica* or mystical union, a *hieros gamos*. They are depicted in a white cosmic egg, two souls now joined as one, like two yolks in one egg (a Gnostic image of spiritual marriage). Certainly the aspect of an incestuous bond is a part of the power of depictions of the Coronation.

It is here that there is a truly 'happy ever after' ending to the Christian story, or, rather, to Christ's ministry on Earth: He resurrects, and then His Mother is assumed into Heaven. The two acts of bodily ascension into Heaven offer the beyond-belief triumph of Christianity. So much of Christian art dwells on the Crucifixion, but here, in these two pictures, *The Transfiguration* and *The Coronation of the Virgin*, joy is allowed to be expressed. These pictures counter the sombreness of so much of Christian art. At the end of a traditional fairy tale, the princess marries the prince, there is a union of male and female, desire and fulfilment, the saved and saviour. It's the same in *The Coronation of the Virgin*: the journey through the challenges of Christ's ministry, one of the central myths of the Western world, is 'rounded off' with a celebration, with joy. After decades of difficulty, there is joy: although the protagonists hardly ever smile in Christian art, the joy is certainly there. It's a joy of release as well as union. Christ ascends to Heaven, and there can be no pain in Heaven. Christ appearing to the humans in *The Transfiguration* is crucially part of this joy, this need to reveal the authentication of joy to humanity.

It's understandable, then, that in Fra Angelico's *The Coronation of the Virgin* this spiritual joy should be conceived in terms of human love, which is always the pattern or basis for religious love. Jesus embraces His Mother (not physically) in Heaven, just as, at the end of the fairy tale or the Hollywood movie, prince and princess, hero and heroine, marry.

The best account of *The Transfiguration* occurs in the 1957 diary of the Romanian 'historian of religions' (his own phrase), Mircea Eliade:

> Of the frescoes that decorate the monks' cells I remember – for reasons other than artistic – the *Transfiguration* and the *Two Marys at the Tomb* (nos. 6 and 8). In these two compositions the Christ is shown to us in his

glory, as though in an immense egg of dazzling whiteness. I feel a limitless admiration for the metaphysical and theological genius of Angelico. In this image of the divine Glory, similar to the Cosmogonic Egg, he says more than could be said in a whole book. The intuition of Angelico is truly stupefying: the light of the transfiguration, which blinded the apostles on Mount Tabor, is the same glorious light of the cosmos on the eve of creation, when the world was still in its embryo state, not yet detached from God.[4]

The Transfiguration is a resplendent image of the truth of the Resurrection. There are too few images of this kind of revelatory power in Renaissance art. The Renaissance exalts the dying man on the Cross: *Crucifixions* far out-number *Transfigurations* or *Resurrections.* Portraying someone in pain and dying is much easier than describing ecstatic transformation, it seems (cinema and television know this only too well – images of suffering out-number images of happiness). What makes Fra Angelico's *Transfiguration* triumphant, then, is not only the triumphalism of Christ's return, but the fact that the painter was able to make it all work. It's an extremely difficult moment to depict successfully.

Rightly, Fra Angelico based his composition on a clear-cut symmetry, with Christ at the centre, completely dominating the scene. His outstretched arms echo the Crucifixion, except he shows that he no longer has wounds in his palms. He faces the viewer directly, calmly, self-assured, not brutally stripped naked now, but clad from neck to toe in soft, clean white robes. Angelico's *Transfiguration* seems so much more satisfying than Raphael Sanzio's over-dramatic, crowded canvas in the Vatican. The light in Fra Angelico's art is all-enveloping – the light is something we keep returning to in the San Marco frescoes. It is an open, limpid light. And it is blinding. Significantly, the saints in the lower third of the picture cower, but the Virgin Mary is the only one who looks directly at the luminous Christ without being overwhelmed by him.

In *The Coronation of the Virgin*, Mary echoes Her pose in so many of Fra Angelico's *Annunciations*: arms crossed on Her chest, leaning forward, staring into space, absorbing the experience of being crowned by the Son of God, who is also Her own son. The Virgin's passive stance is exactly that of Angelico's many *Annunciations*, ever the receiver of masculine power, ever the passive one receiving what the active one does. Even as She is being crowned Queen of Heaven, She is humble and subdued by the greater power and divinity of Her son. The atmosphere in the Coronation event of majesty and triumph is countered in Angelico's version by a tranquillity and humility in the attitude of the Virgin. Even in Her ecstasy She is quiet, contemplative, submissive. Even in Her moment of glory, to be welcomed into Heaven *bodily*, She is humble, deferring attention away from Herself, towards Christ.

It's an amazing touch, this humility of the Virgin, that, even though She is the *Mother* of God, She should still have to kneel *below* Him, still have to submit *Herself* to *Him*. It's amazing because one might expect the Son in Renaissance art to bow low before the Mother, to make a show of respect for his parent(s). But no, this is theology and religion, not psychology and sociology. Christ always has people at His feet, people are always below Him: the followers looking up to Him being crucified; soldiers below Christ in Piero della Francesca's *Resurrection* (1460); Mary Magdalene stretching to touch His feet in so many *Noli Me Tangere* paintings (Titian's is a famous one [1511-12]; Fra Angelico includes a *Noli Me Tangere* in cell number 1 at San Marco).⁵ Besides, it's theologically tricky for Christ to submit to the Virgin, because, as God, He is the father of the Virgin and the Creator of all. Christ is the Son *and* the Father, that's part of the mystery of Christianity.

✳

These lines I wrote on a visit to San Marco Museum in 1991 (when I was in a particularly poetic state of mind): *The Last Supper* (1446) at San Marco features windows with views exactly the same as those outside the windows of the cell. The implication is that the space of the painting and the space of 'real life' are entwined. These divine mysteries are happening right here, right now. That is what Fra Angelico wants to communicate. Not over there, or in the church, but here, in your own cell, your own house, your own bedroom. Open your eyes and the Mystery will be before you. Everywhere you look, you'll see the Mystery. Close your eyes at night, and you will partake of the Passion. Mystery is everywhere.

Each fresco has a creamy background – the same colour (almost) as the wall. One blends into the other. The inner, sacred field of mystery, and the outer world of secular affairs merge. Sacred and secular enmesh. The mysteries contained in the picture spill out into the cell. The creamy white expands. The egg of the Transfiguration is hatched. Rebirth is beginning – rebirth is happening – right now, right here.

Rebirth is to be wondered at, but it's going on all the time. Fra Angelico cuts out the junk. He excises everything but glory from his works. His images sing of glory, they come forth from The Glory. They are The Glory made flesh.

This line of cells, with the wooden beams above, the arched doorways, the bare walls, their regularity – they are spaces in which to be alone – to be absolutely alone – with oneself, with one's body, with one's spirituality. Nothing must intervene. The rhythms of the day and night predominate. Sunlight does the illuminating. Nights would be very dark here, as everywhere in the mediæval world. The San Marco cells are not unlike Buddhist spaces. The means are different in Eastern and Occidental monasteries, but the aim is the same: total glory.

VII

Ecstasy and Pain:
Crucifixions, Revelations
and Other Works

FRA BEATO ANGELICO PAINTED a variety of subjects, not only Madonna and Child or Crucifixion images, though these remain the subjects of his greatest works. One of the pleasures of visiting Rome is to leave the trail in the Vatican that leads towards Michelangelo Buonarroti's Sistine Chapel ceiling, which seems always to be thronged with tourists (for a good reason, though), and step into the private Chapel of Nicholas V. This space is one of the sanctuaries in the otherwise over-crowded Vatican. Paintings of Fra Angelico's such as *St Lawrence Distributing Alms to the Poor and the Infirm* (c. 1447-50) is, like the picture of Christ being mocked in Florence's San Marco, a panoply of hands, all out-stretched, hoping for something from the saint.

One of Fra Angelico's most celebrated works is his San Marco *Descent From the Cross*, completed around 1440. Here Angelico demonstrates his control of a large collection of figures, several saints and *beati* (the beatified). The tri-arched frame contains Angelico's harmony of blues and reds in the costumes standing in a rich green landscape. There are one or two kneeling figures (such as the Magdalene tending Christ's feet), but the majority of the figures are standing stiffly upright. The rigidity of the characters serves to emphasize the slumped limbs of the dead God. As in *Depositions* and *Pietàs* of painters such as Rogier van der Weyden or Petrus Christus, the limp outstretched arms of Christ help to make the painting emotionally dynamic. Christ's awkward, diagonal body creates plangent tensions in the *Pietàs* and *Descents* of the Renaissance. The gestures of the participants are at once spontaneous, momentary, and eternal, as in Leonardo da Vinci's *Last Supper*. The gestural energy is counter-balanced by a frieze-like stasis, which seems to make the spiritual agony and silent suffering even more piercing. This is distinctly a human tragedy, too, this *Descent From the Cross*, for the bright reds and blues of the costumes do not look like a part of nature at all. Nature is shown as cool green and brown, while the humans are gaudy. Humanity and its arcane rituals stand out from nature as unreal.

One of Fra Angelico's most moving Crucifixion scenes is the *predella* painting from the *San Marco Altarpiece* (1438-40) which depicts a *Lamentation* scene. As in the *Man of Sorrows* fresco (1441) in the cloister of San Marco Museum, simple symmetry does much of the work of expressionism here: on either side of the dead Christ is a woman: the Virgin Mary on one side, Mary Magdalene on the other. They are holding the wounded hands. The Magdalene leans down to kiss his hand. The two women mirror each other, one as the dead man's mother, the other as his potential lover. They stand on a little field sprinkled with many flowers. Behind the rock is a pale blue sky. Christ stands on the winding sheet, moments before being wrapped in it and placed in the sepulchre. The tomb itself is a large rectangular structure carved out of a huge rock. It is utterly black in there: the darkness is ready to swallow the dead God. Christ appears as the Man of Sorrows; he is displayed as an object of contemplation, presented to the viewer by the senior figure in *Pietà* scenes, Joseph of Arimathea (or it may be Nicodemus). Christ's body is openly displayed, the arms wide, the frame placed frontally to the viewer.

Christ's pose recreates the outstretched arms and bowed head of the Crucifixion, but here he is tended by friends and followers. Instead of the horror of Golgotha, with its barren rocks, skulls and bones, this is a flowery mead, as in Fra Angelico's *Annunciations*. There is a liturgical base to the painting, linking it with the Eucharist and the eucharistic body of Jesus (W. Hood, 110). Fra Angelico's *Lamentation* is above all a superb meditation on the Passion. Few other paintings so poignantly describe the tenderness of Christ's followers, the way they mourned him, and delicately tended him.

✳

Fra Angelico's *Crucifixion* (1420) in the Metropolitan Museum of Art in New York City is, like the *Crucifixions* of Masaccio, set against a gold ground. A series of figures below the Cross act out their feelings with hieratic gestures. The colours are faded, but still the emotion of the painting persists. Here, one of the Marys, probably the Magdalene, kneels before the Cross, her arms upraised in woe. It is these violent gestures, these demonstrations of emotion, that make Renaissance painting so powerful. Without these exaggerated displays of feeling, Renaissance art would come across as a cool, distanced art. Perhaps this would be a good thing. But we prize Renaissance art for its shows of emotion, its emotional sensitivity and subtlety. Fra Angelico is powerful partly because he puts such feelings into his art. The New York *Crucifixion* is one of those Quattrocento works which reduces emotion to a series of simple but powerful gestures. The Magdalene with her hands raised; other saints praying; and the Virgin standing impassively, Her arms folded over Her chest, looking not up at Her son, but off into the distance.

Another *Crucifixion*, similar in format to the Metropolitan Museum piece, is the Fogg Art Museum *Crucifix With Cardinal Torquemada* (1446). Again there is the Cross set in a rock which, as in many of Fra Angelico's *Crucifixions*, resembles the bole of a tree (a Cross-wood-tree-rock axis fits symbolically, of course).

Fra Angelico's *Saint Dominic With the Crucifix* is an unusual treatment of the subject in Angelico's art, and in Renaissance art. What Angelico has done is to strip the image down to its fundamental components. Background is reduced to an abstract blue round and a white space which does for the Earth. The wooden Cross and Christ on it dominates the painting. At the base of the Cross is a rock, but there is nothing else in the landscape to suggest time or place. Kneeling at the base of the Cross is the saint who dominates San Marco theologically, Saint Dominic. His face is expresses grief, humility, an intense identification with the dying God on the Cross. The viewer is invited to look through Saint Dominic's eyes at Christ: Saint Dominic is meant to be the mediator between Jesus and the viewer. Angelico's reduction to just the figures against the abstract background emphasizes the intensity and psychology of the subject. There is no landscape or city or other figures to distract from the central drama. The generalized blue and sandy-coloured setting looks forward to the abstraction of paintings such as Diego Velásquez' *Christ Crucified* (1631-32, Prado, Madrid), which shows the Saviour against a jet black background. At the same time, there is a realism about the figures, which contrasts with the abstraction of their setting. They are intended to be real people, really suffering in front of the viewer.

'Piercing' is both literal and metaphoric in Fra Angelico's San Marco frescoes. Piercing in the emotional and spiritual sense, and in the literal sense of the spear entering Christ's side, which is depicted in cell number 42. So abhorrent is this mutilation of the Son of God that one of the women, probably His mother, turns away, covering her face in grief. Fra Angelico depicts a terrifying abjection from which there seems to be no release. The soft pastel tones modulate but do not dissipate the intensity of the sorrow. As in other frescoes, the blood dripping from Christ's wounds is prominent: it runs down the Cross, onto the rocks below, spreading towards the Roman centurion, the kneeling saint, the grieving women, and the viewer. In a workshop version of *Saint Dominic With the Crucifix* (in cell 21, an inferior version of the Fra Angelico painting in the cloisters), the blood does not just run down the Cross onto the rock at the base, it drips profusely from the wounds in Christ's palms, and spurts from the hole in his side. The North dormitory *Saint Dominic With the Crucifix* is not the only bloody depiction of the subject – there is one in cells 15, 16, 17, 18 and 21, among others.

Christianity certainly is an eye-opener. The image of this grown, saintly man kneeling in melancholy and humility before another grown man, who's naked, nailed to a Cross and bleeding copiously, might be baffling to visitors from other cultures or other planets. What is going on here? It is bewildering. Even more bewildering, though, is the fresco in cell number twenty, which shows Saint Dominic, esteemed founder of the order and the monastery, stripped to the waist and flagellating himself. It certainly is odd to see a grown half-naked man whipping himself in front of a dying naked man. The vanity of humanity knows no bounds, it seems. Or is it humility?

The large, thronged *Crucifixion* fresco (1438) in the chapter room of San Marco Museum contains many images of grieving. There are no soldiers or proletariat here who jeer and mock the dying deity, as in *Crucifixions* by Hieronymous Bosch or Quentin Massys. Instead, Fra Angelico's painting is a parade of pain displayed through muted colours and fluttering, spread hands. Some figures clasp their hands, together; other clasp their eyes; others hold their hands up in despair; some kneel and pray, hands clasped together; others point significantly; and others wring their hands wearily. Below the chapter house *Crucifixion* there is a long line of saints and dignitaries, shown in little round paintings. We see their heads and shoulders – and their hands, which bless, grasp books, hold pens and staffs.

The most moving section of the large *Crucifixion* is the group of figures to the left of Christ. The three Marys and St John console each other. But the Mother of God is so overcome she faints, as in many Early Netherlandish *Crucifixions* (such as Rogier van der Weyden's stunning *Descent From the Cross*). In Rogier van der Weyden's Prado, Madrid painting, the Virgin's slumped, curved pose emulates exactly the exhausted body of Christ as it is lowered down from the Cross. Rogier brilliantly shows how the Virgin Mary suffered the same pain as Her son.

Fra Angelico does the same: his Virgin Mary falls backwards, Her arms outstretched on either side, exactly as in pictures of the *Pietà*, *Lamentation* or *Entombment*. The Madonna's collapsed posture recalls Fra Angelico's own *Lamentation* from the *predella* of the *San Marco Altarpiece*.

Not only is the collapsing posture of the Virgin Mary a clever invention, but in front of Her the Magdalene kneels, arms thrown around the Madonna, experiencing similar griefs, simultaneously physically supporting the Virgin, expressing solidarity with Her, and lost in her own sorrow. While St John stands beside the Virgin Mary looking suitably concerned and sad, it is the women who show the full strength of their emotions, in this *Crucifixion* and in most *Crucifixions*. It is the women who physically collapse, arms flailing, eyes streaming, mouths open in silent screams. It is an inspired composition, this group of the three Marys and St John. Seen close to, the colours of the dresses of the three Marys – yellow, pink, red, blue, green – are surprisingly bright and cheerful, especially when compared to the sombre browns and greens and greys of the gathering of (entirely male) bishops and saints on the right hand side of the painting.

As one tours the Dominican priory of San Marco, moving quietly from the cloisters, through the chapter rooms, arcades, the beautiful colonaded library to the upper dormitories and cells, one is struck by the sheer number of Passion scenes, of *Crucifixions* and scenes of suffering. Yet, strange to relate, the effect really is not overwhelming and depressing. It might be. A monastery full of *Crucifixions* might be a horrible experience, with its depictions of unrelenting pain. Yet Fra Angelico's San Marco paintings are not sickening or saddening. The opposite.

Also, one is not over-awed by the sheer amount of visual material to consider. Most rooms contain a fresco or a painting or three to consume, but one does not feel inundated. Perhaps it is precisely because most of the frescoes and paintings revolve around the same subject, it makes them appear unified, and their consumption is a very satisfying experience. We see Fra Angelico revolving the same basic feeling of suffering and sanctity, holiness and humility, again and again. These feelings expresses themselves on the one hand in the quiet, humble Madonnas, either with the child, or awaiting the Annunciation; and on the other in the great series of *Crucifixions* and Passion scenes.

✳

Other images from the descent into hell of the Passion of Christ include the workshop *Christ Bound to the Column,* in cell 26. The self-flagellating St Dominic kneels in the foreground, with the sitting Virgin Mary as another exemplar. This is an image for meditation on the Christian notions of suffering and redemption through divine power. It is not like the usual illustrations of a particular scene – there are no soldiers beating up Jesus, for a start, and the Saviour has no marks on him.

Fra Angelico in his San Marco Museum frescoes does not illustrate every stage in the Passion as it is described in the *Gospels*; rather, he chooses certain emotions or states to depict. He extracts the key feelings or religious acts of the Passion and enshrines them in sparse, luminous settings. Instead of the 'realistic' settings of later Renaissance painters, such as Raphael Sanzio, Andrea del Sarto and Andrea Mantegna, who made sure their landscapes and interiors looked like 'real' places, with all the right features in all the right places, Angelico takes the figures and puts them in a neutral setting where they can stand out. The humanity, irony, tenderness and pain of the *Gospel* events is foregrounded even as the figures themselves are foregrounded in Angelico's frescoes.

Thus, *The Mocking of Christ*, in cell 7, 'telescopes a number of narrative episodes stretched over a long period of time into a single and remarkably non-dramatic image', as William Hood put it (216). *The Mocking of Christ* features those disembodied hands and faces which prove so effective. Here the fact that Christ is blindfolded, as well as wearing the crown of thorns, exaggerates the savagery of the mockery of the hands and faces. Hands and sticks and floating faces also appear in the *Homo Pietatis* or *Man of Sorrows* (cell 27), which is a jumble of motifs from the Passion: Jesus and the sepulchre, a cross behind him, a lance on the left, a column on the right, and the mocking people. Some of the frescoes are like summaries of *Gospel* events, or meditations upon a group of actions. Thus Fra Angelico presents a spiritual journey through the Christian story, not a stage by stage, blow by blow record of it.

✳

Other frescoes at the San Marco Museum in Florence which share the same mysterious, soft, limpid light include *The Presentation in the Temple*, *The Piercing of Christ's Side*, *Noli Me Tangere*, and of course the

Annunciation in cell number 3. *The Presentation in the Temple* (1425-30) is a particularly lyrical painting. In a Micheozzan niche stand Simeon, who holds Jesus, Joseph, the Virgin, the kneeling St Peter Martyr and a woman sometimes identified as the prophetess Anna, sometimes as the Blessed Villana de' Botti. This is one of Fra Angelico's happiest paintings – or one of his least painful. Joseph nearly smiles, though most of the participants are as solemn as usual in Angelico's (and Renaissance) art. The Christ child, swaddled as tightly as he is in *Presentations* by Giovanni Bellini and Andrea del Mantegna, is utterly expressionless as he stares at the patriarch who cradles him gently.

✳ ✳ ✳

Fra Giovanni Beato Angelico da Fiesole's art endures because he miraculously pinpoints and expresses eternal and invaluable aspects of what it means to be human: humility, devotion, perseverance, courage, spiritual feelings, and love. And his form of expression is so lyrical, so sweet, so subtle, and so elaborate. Angelico is a great artist because he delivers everything a great artist should – *and more.*

Fra Angelico's art goes beyond greatness: it has a beauty and spirit that seems to have always been present. Like the work of the finest artists, it's as if Angelico's paintings have always existed. They come into the world fully formed – a mysterious birth into plenitude.

Illustrations

Works by Fra Angelico

and Fra Angelico and his contemporaries.

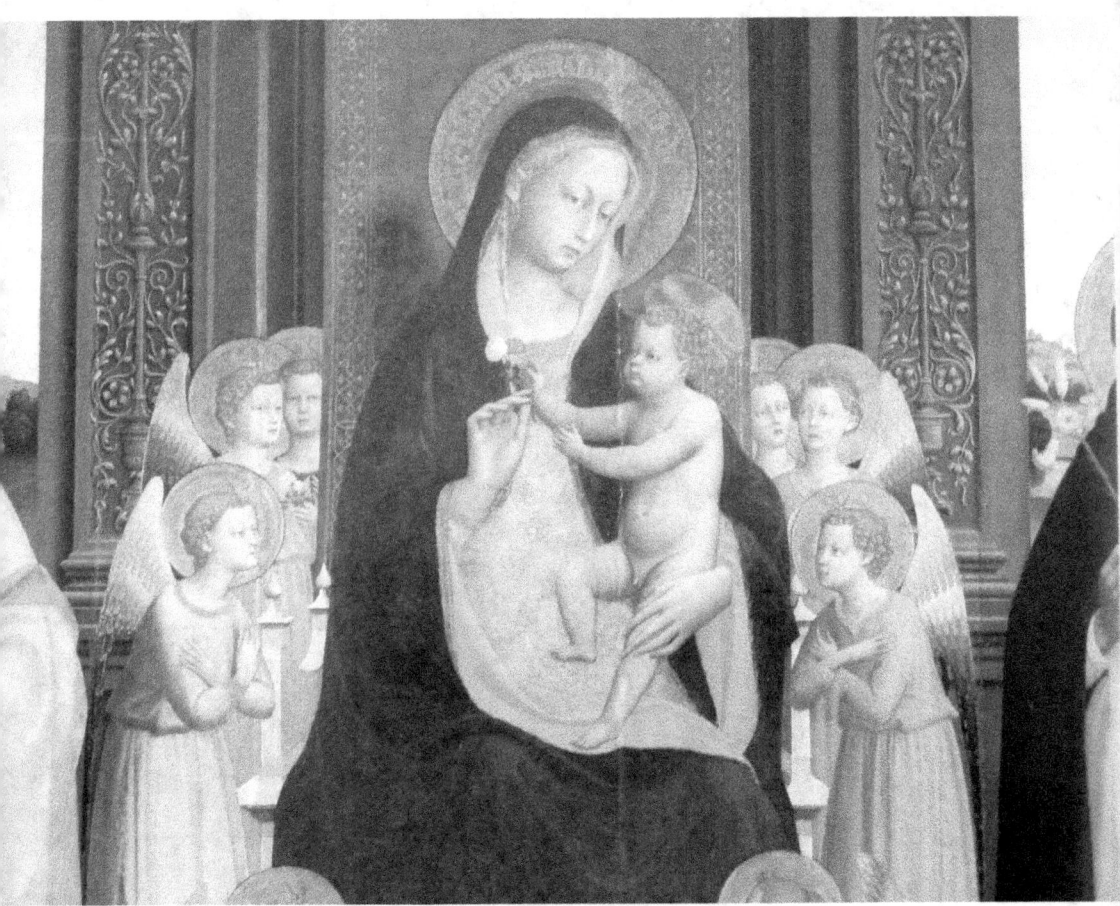

Fra Angelico, Virgin and Child, Fiesole

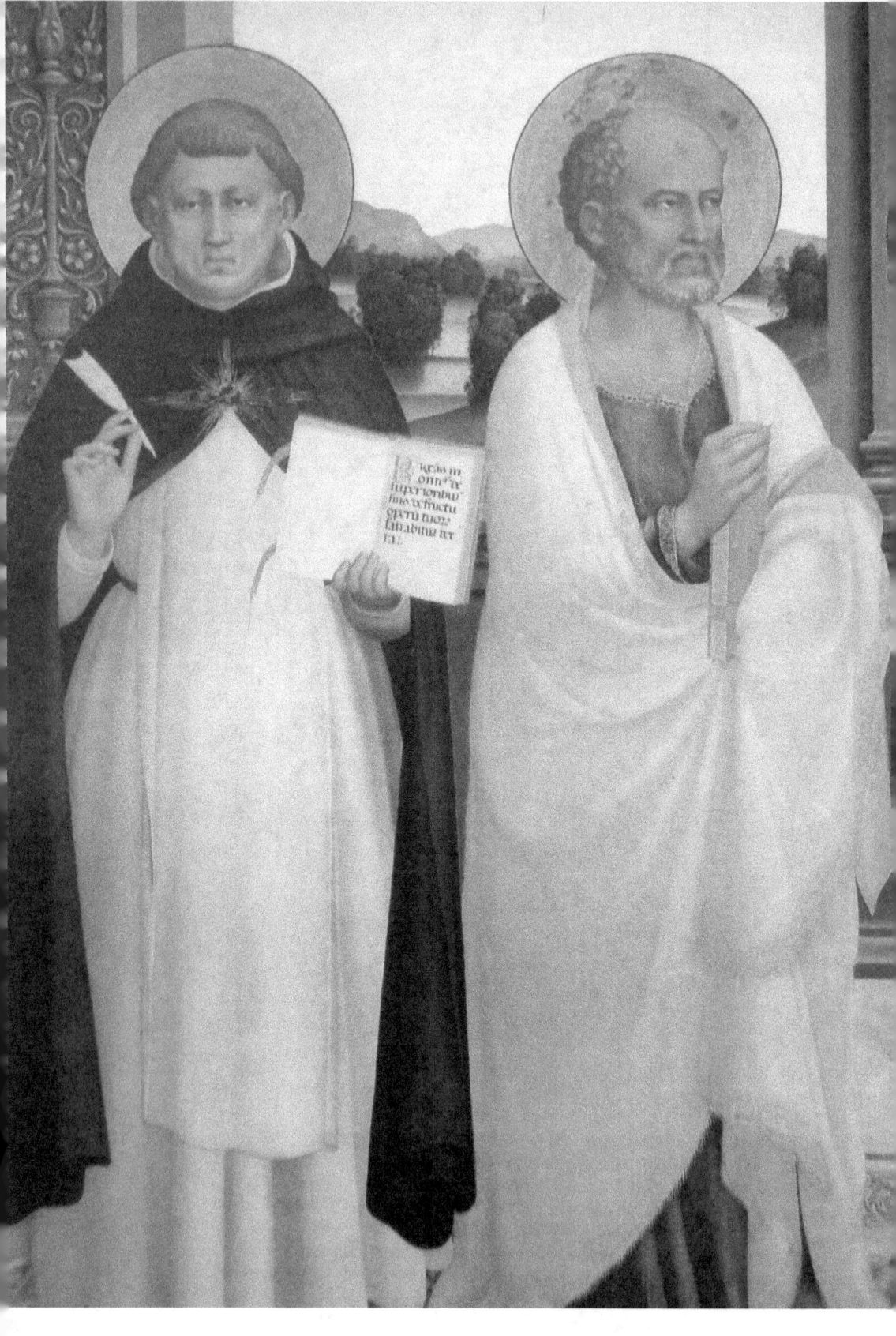

Fra Angelico, Virgin and Child Enthroned, c. 1424-25, detail, Fiesole

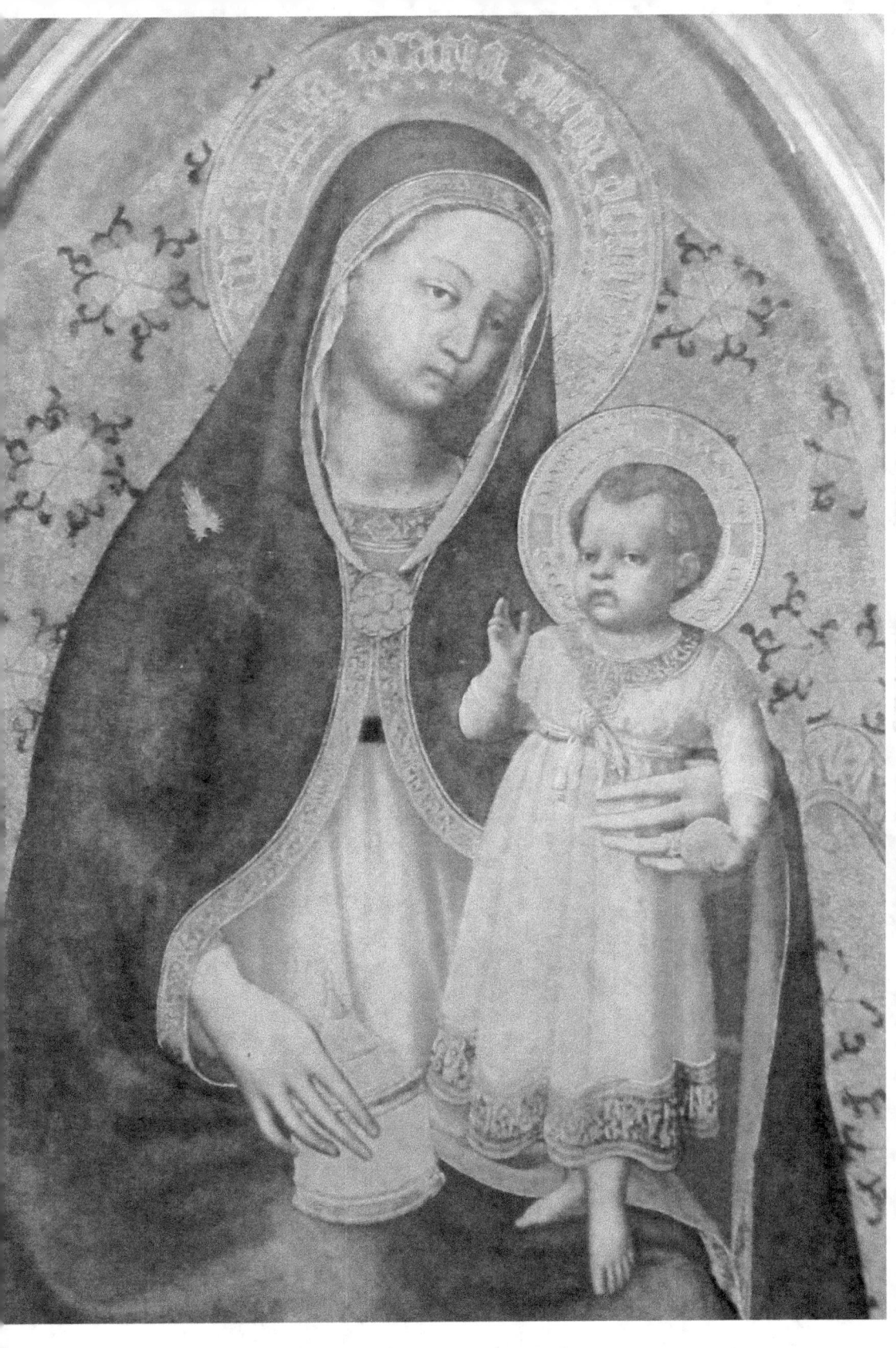

Fra Angelico, San Pier Martire Altarpiece

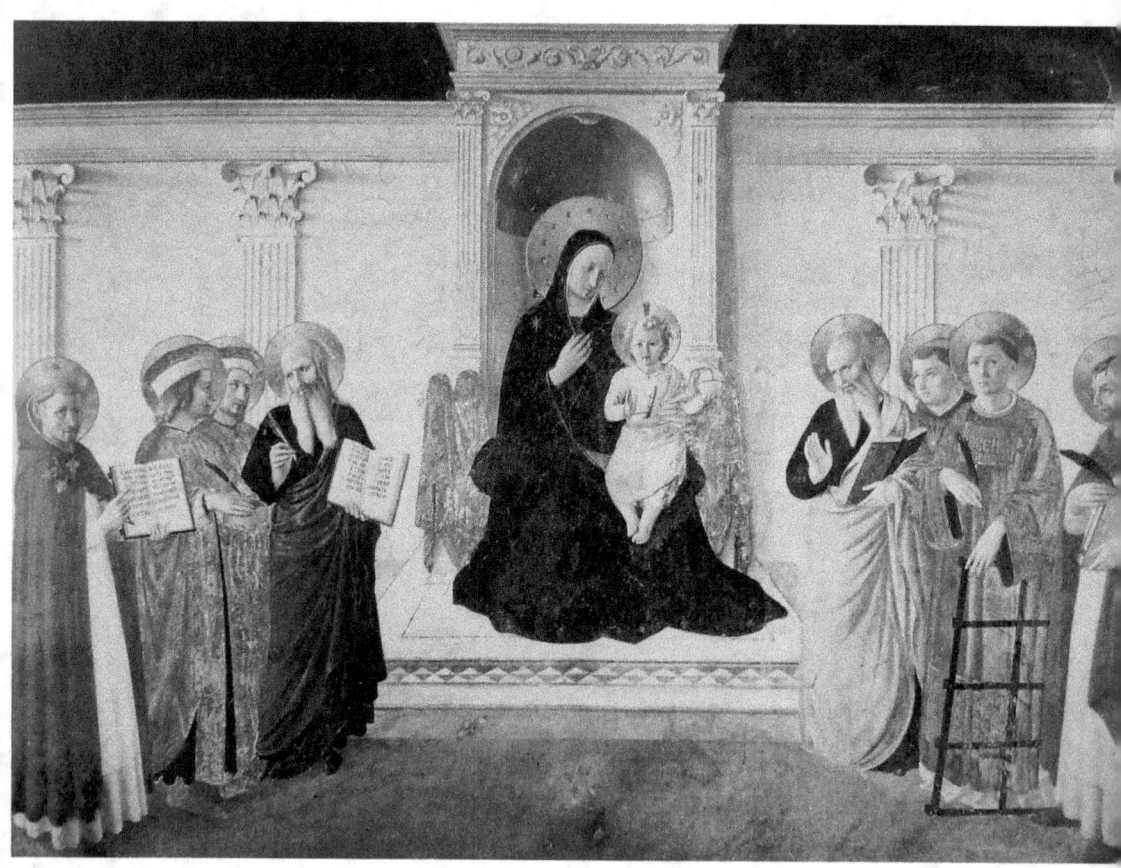

Fra Angelico, Sacra Conversazione, 1440

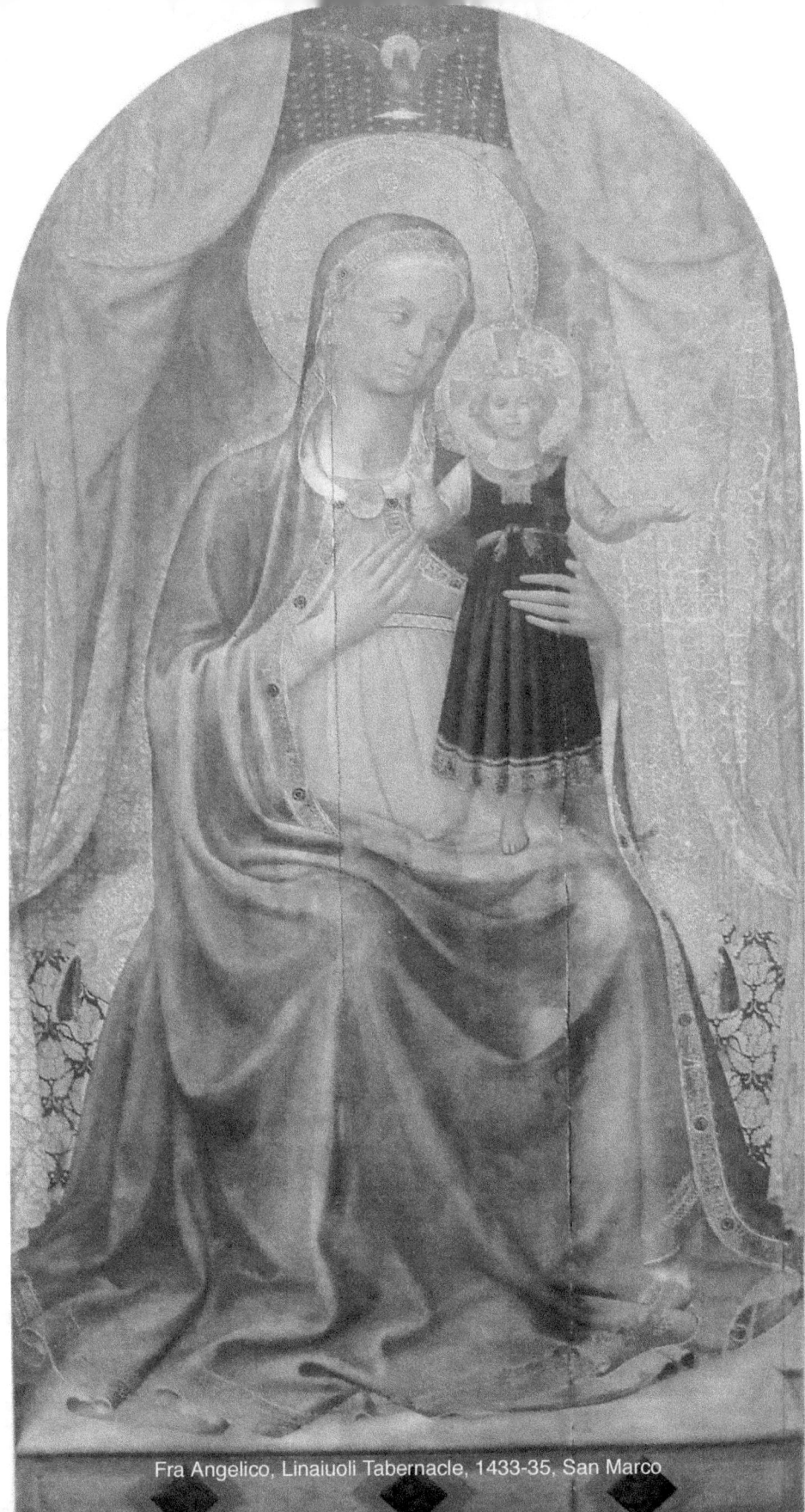

Fra Angelico, Linaiuoli Tabernacle, 1433-35, San Marco

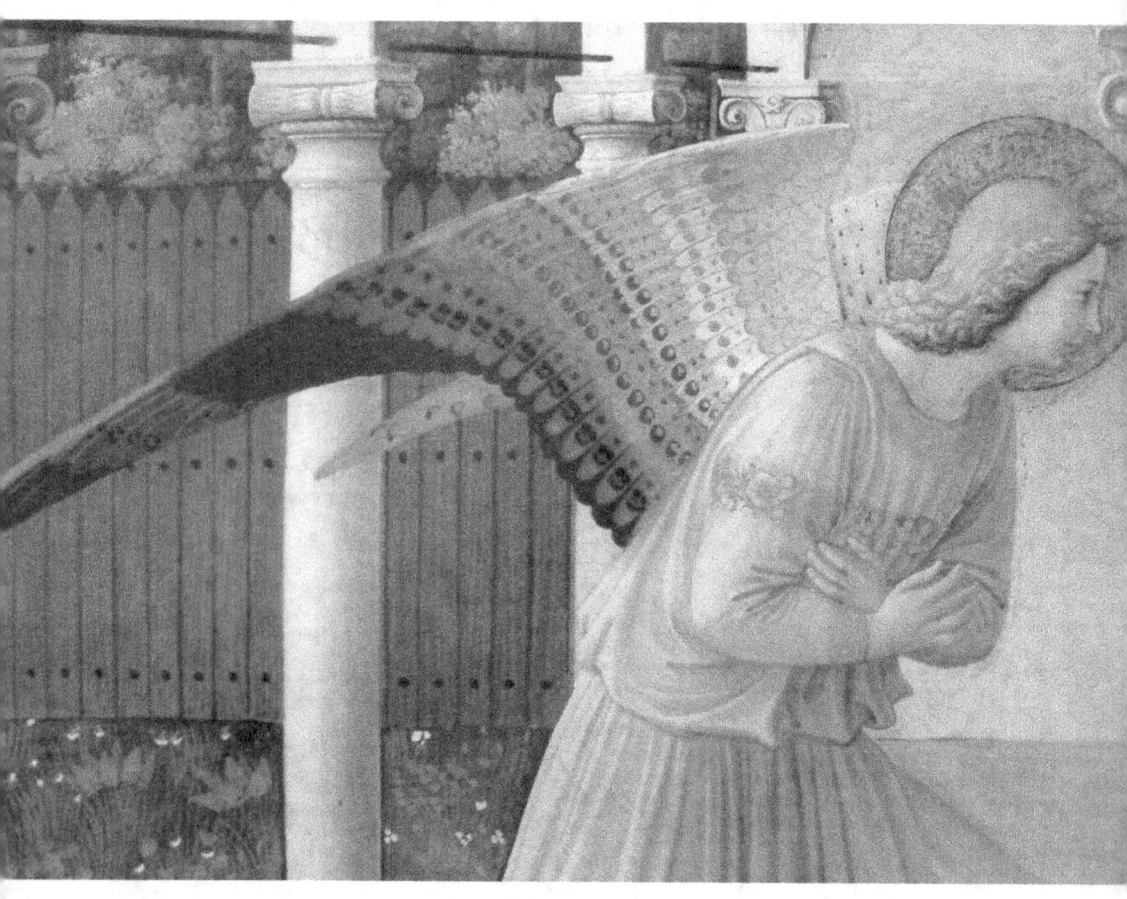

Fra Angelico, Annunciation, c. 1450, detail, upper corridor, San Marco

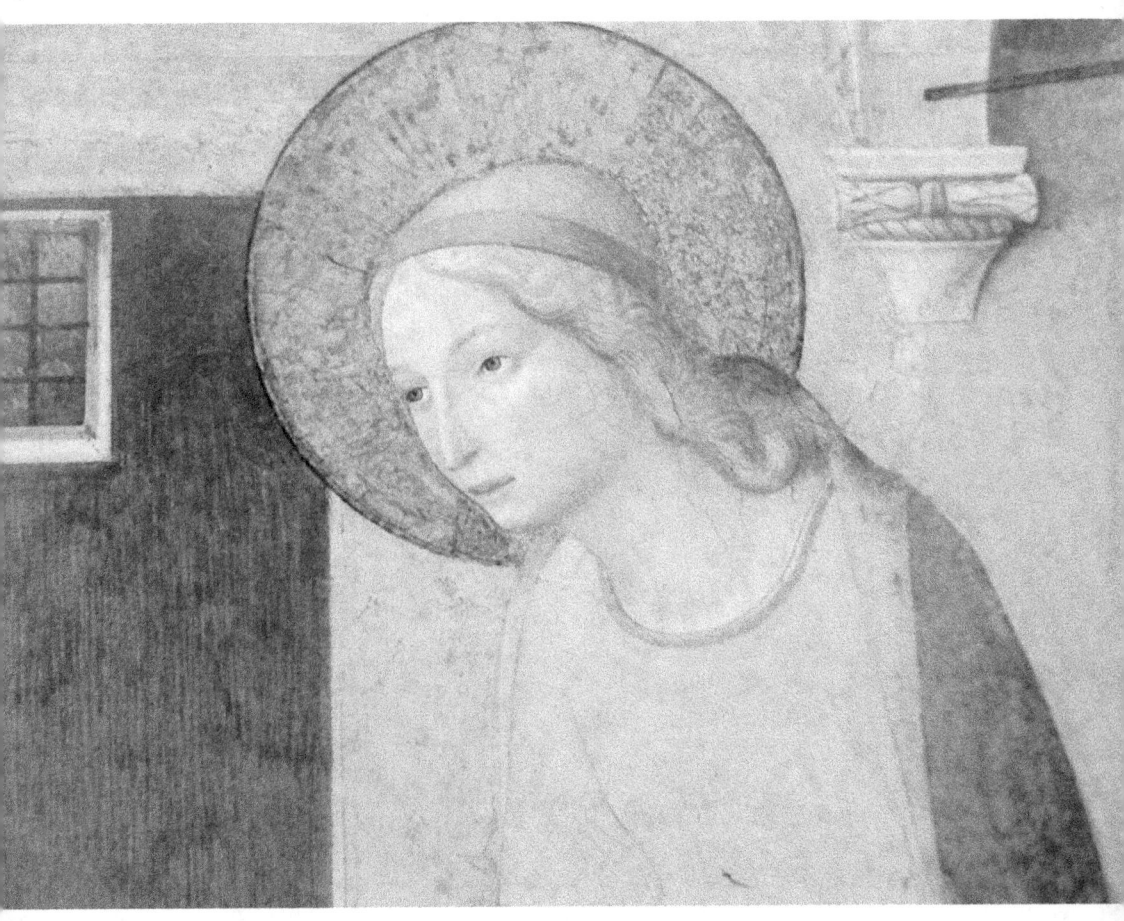

Fra Angelico, Annunciation, detail, San Marco, Florence

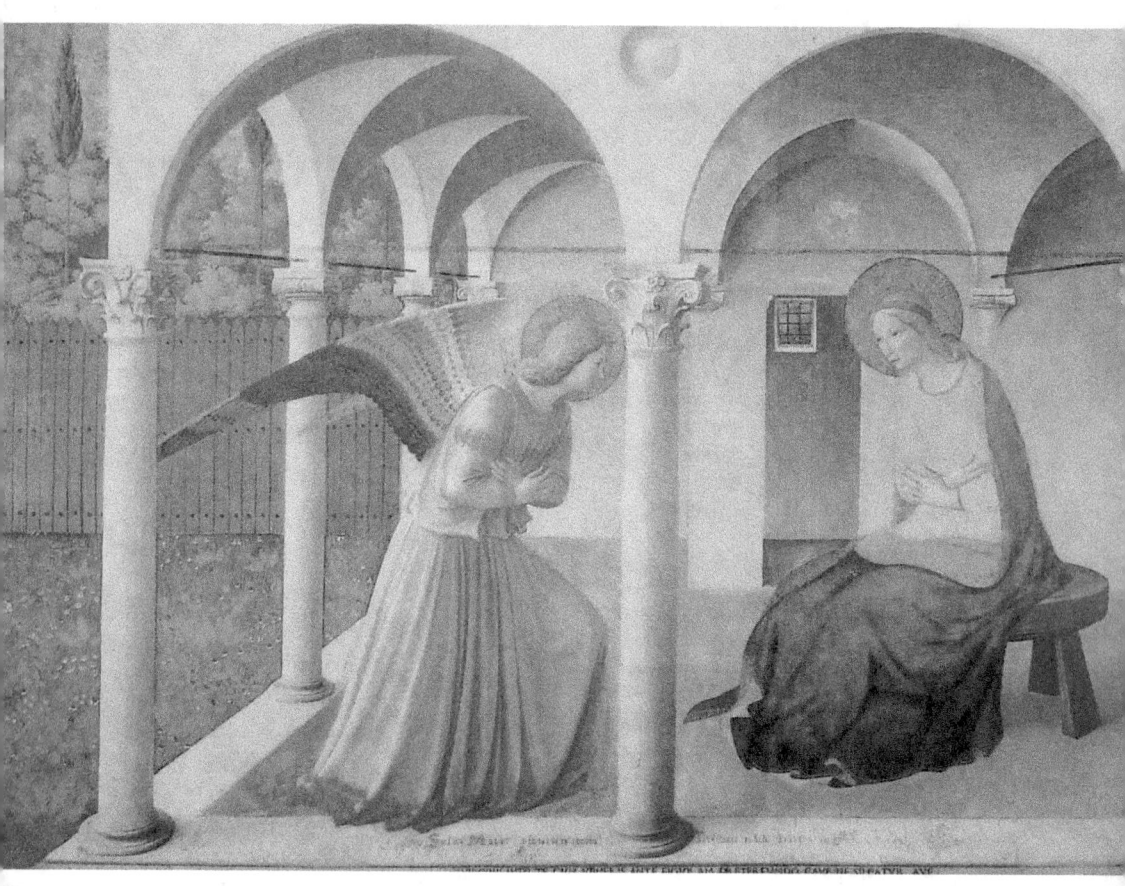

Fra Angelico, The Annunciation, San Marco, Florence

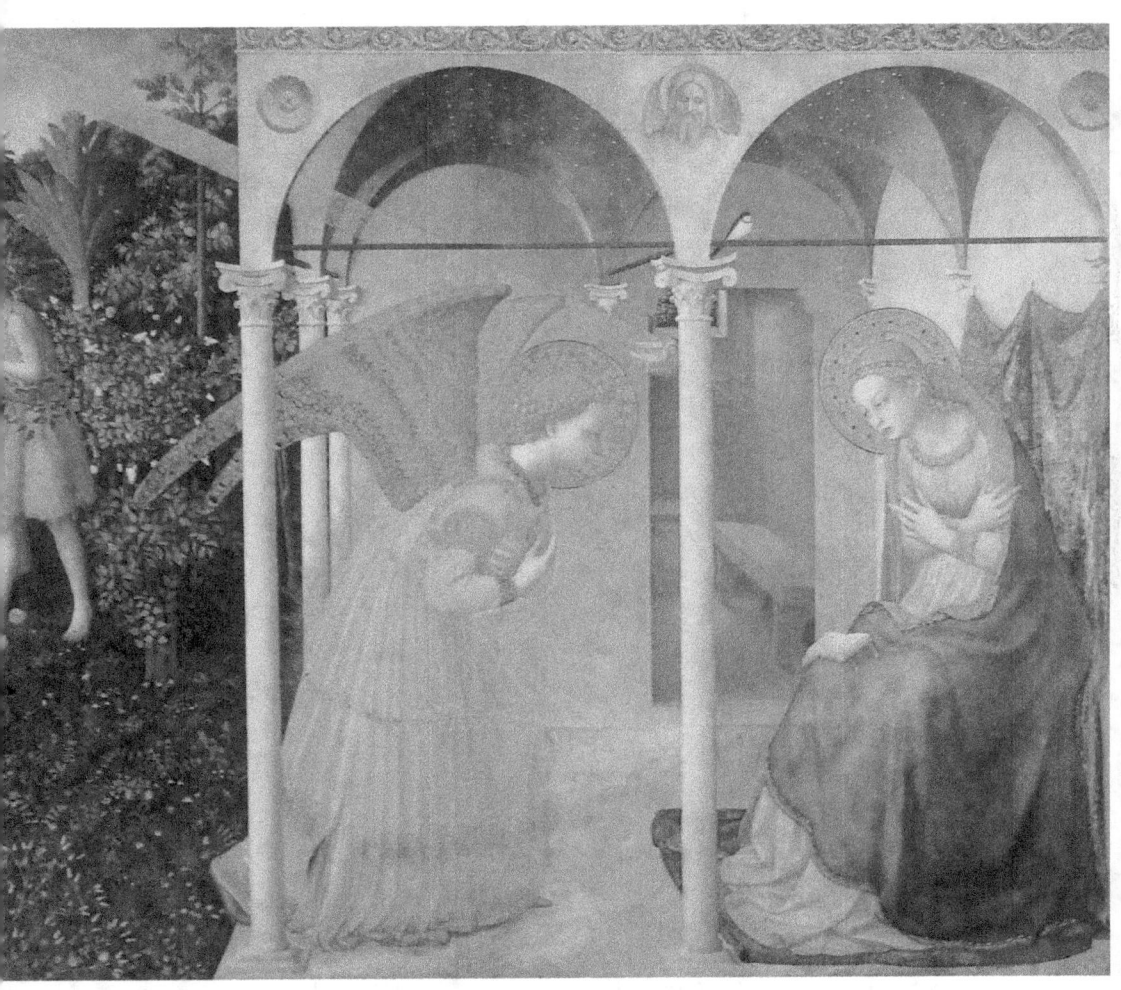

Fra Angelico, Annunciation, Prado, Madrid

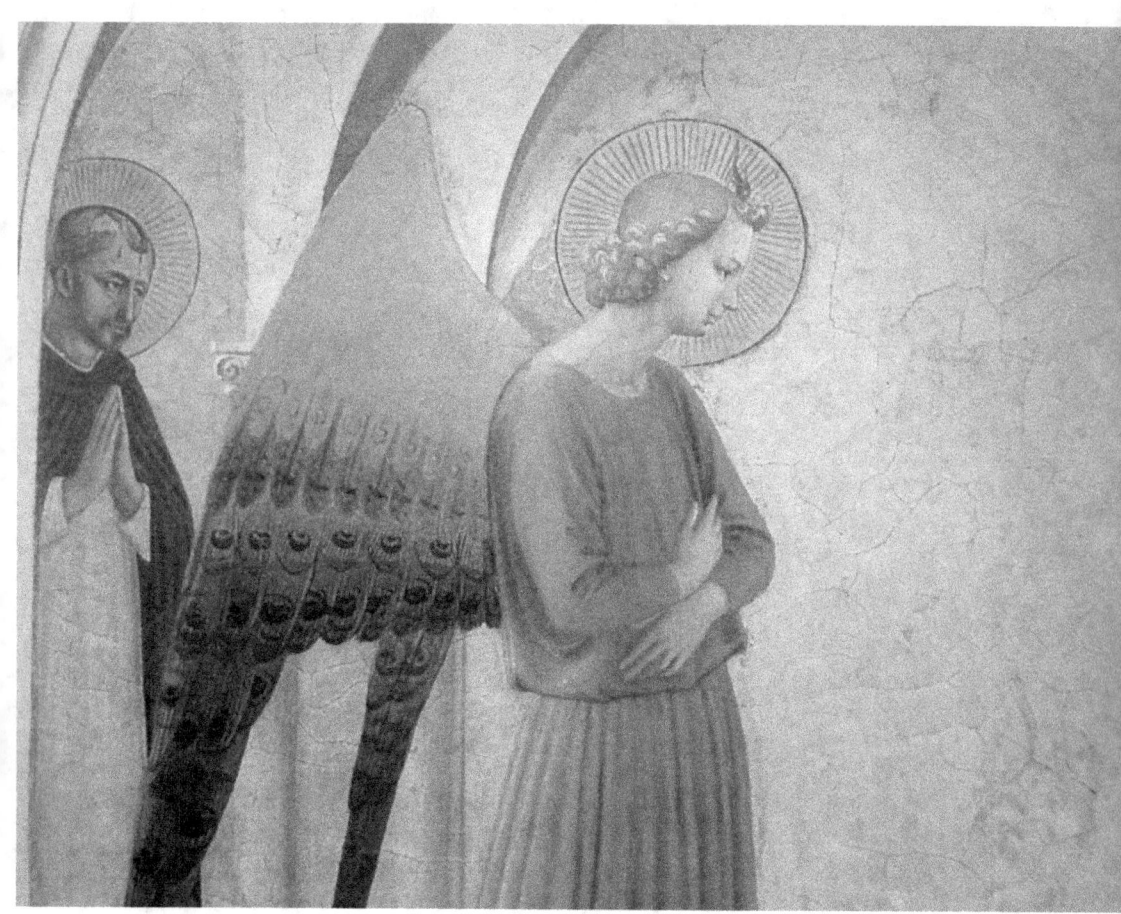

Fra Angelico, Annunciation, cell 3, San Marco

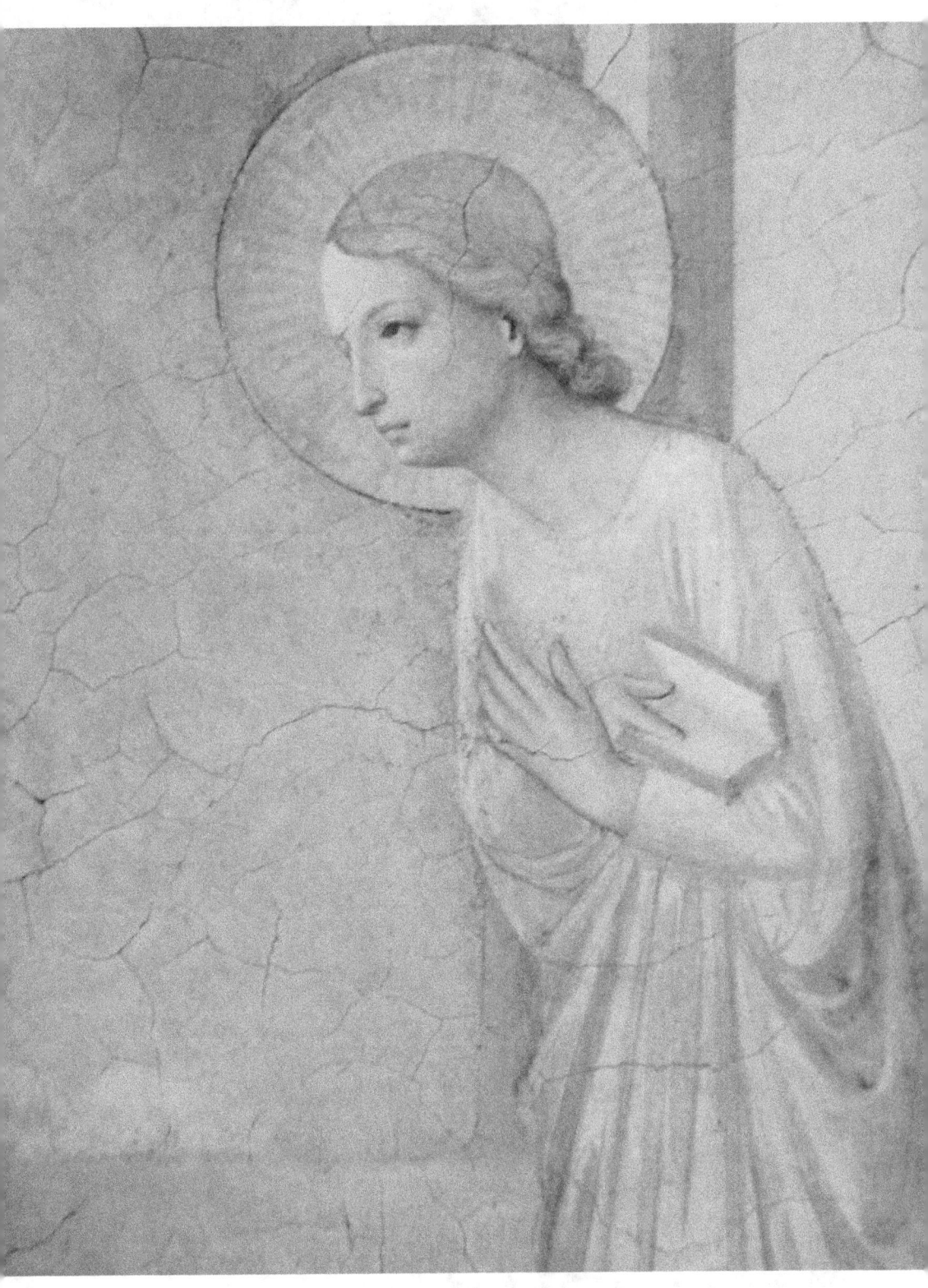

Fra Angelico, Annunciation, cell 3 at San Marco

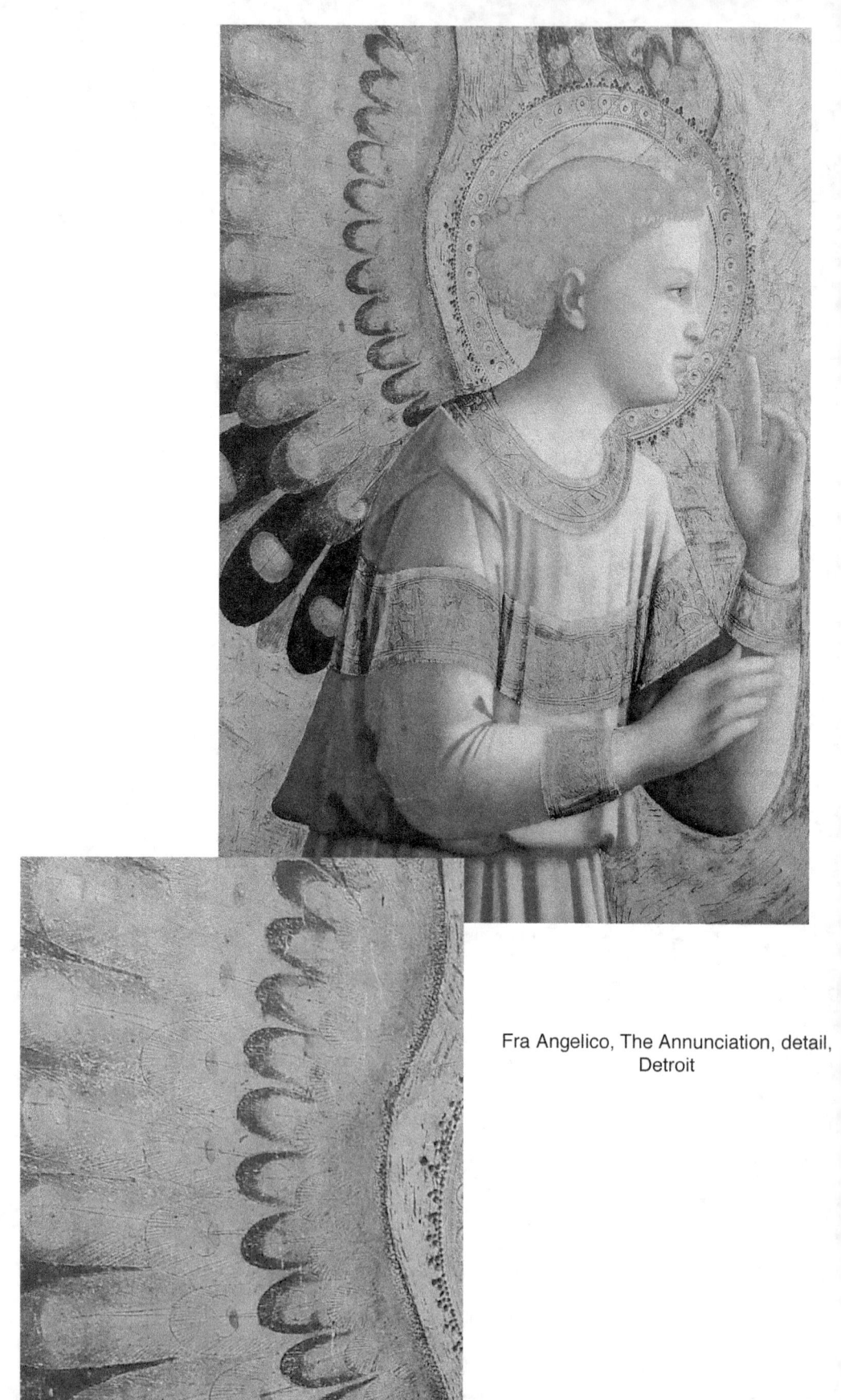

Fra Angelico, The Annunciation, detail, Detroit

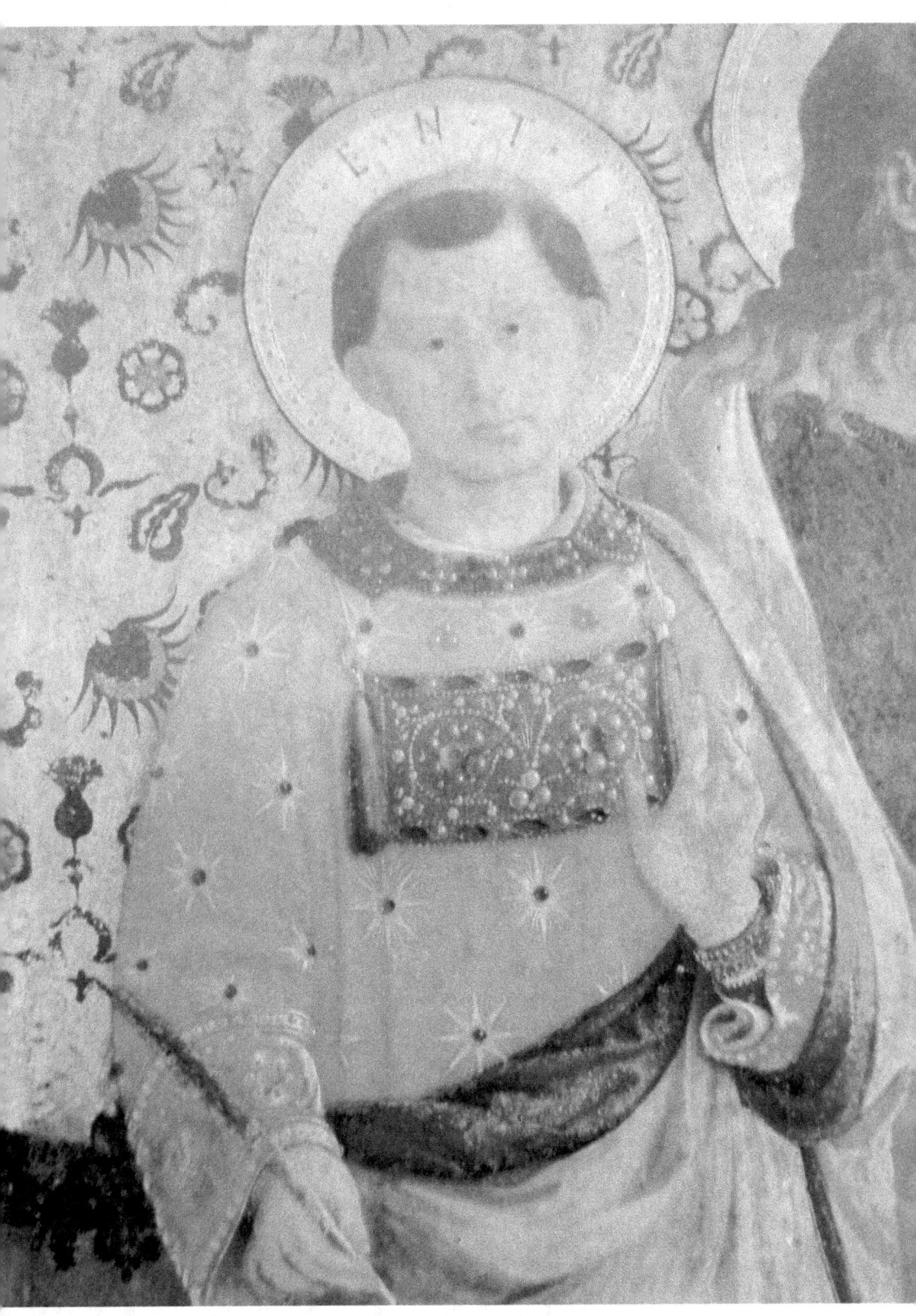

Fra Angelico, San Marco Altarpiece, 1438-40, detail

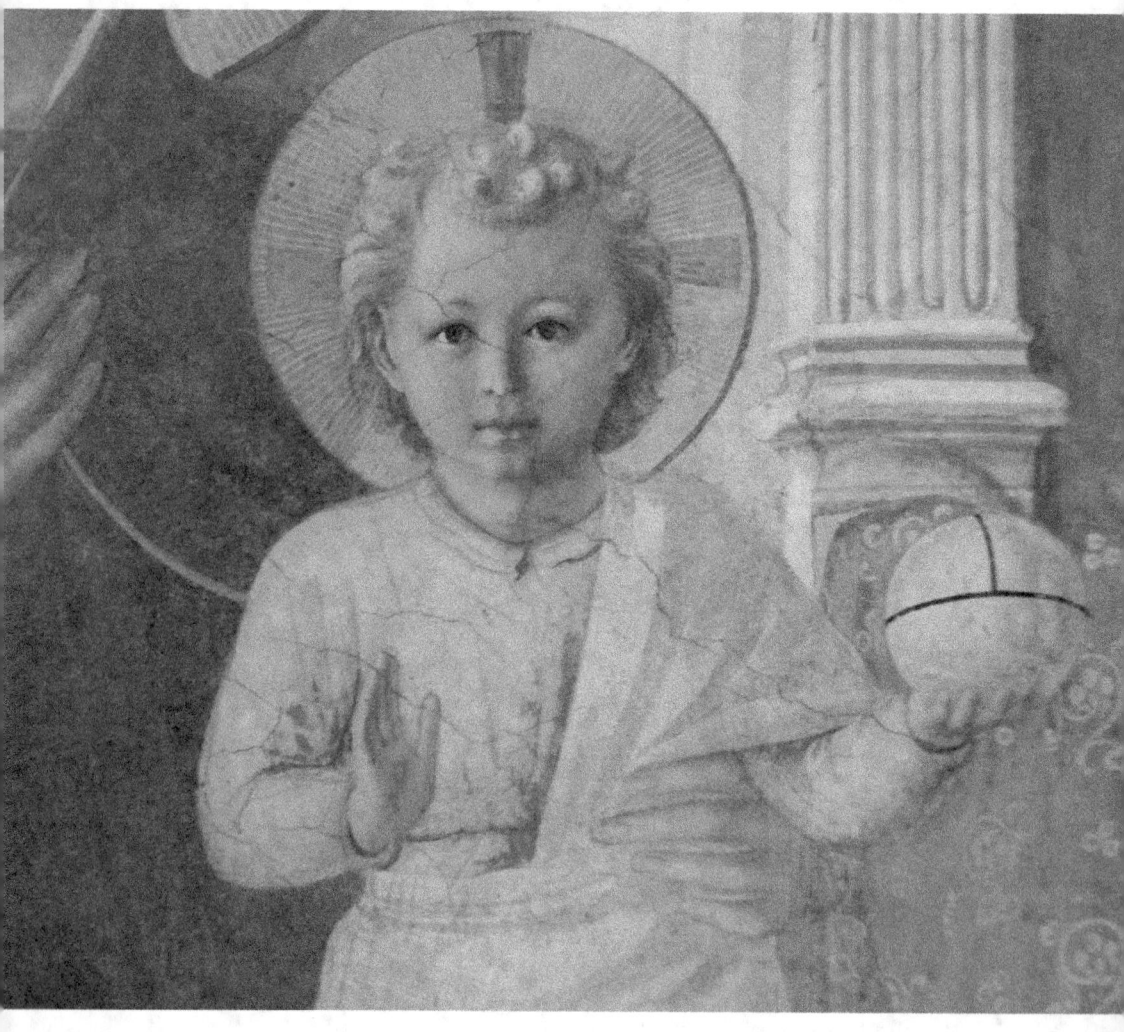

Fra Angelico, Virgin and Child Enthroned, c. 1450, detail, San Marco

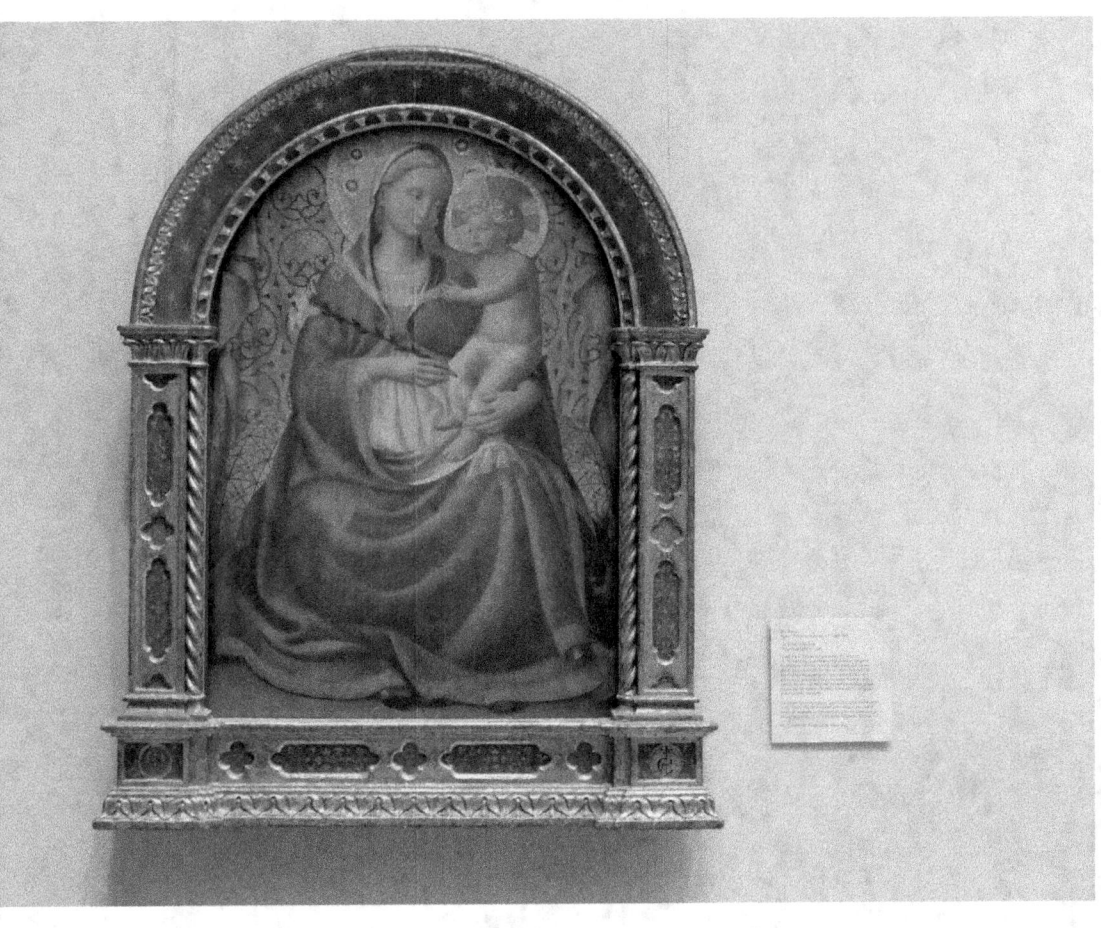

Fra Angelico, Madonna and Child, Metropolitan Museum of Art, New York

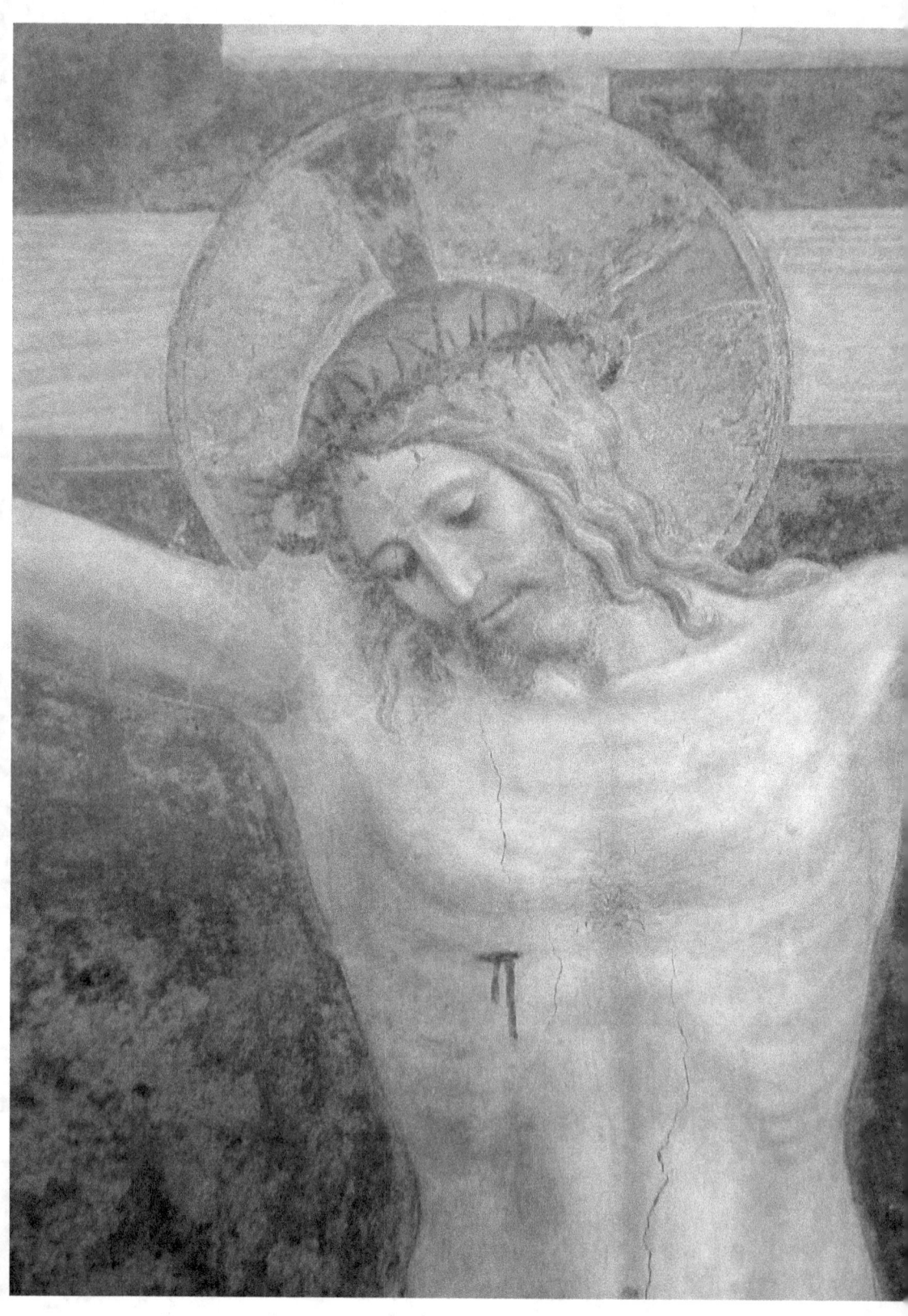

Fra Angelico, Christ On the Cross, c. 1442, detail, San Marco

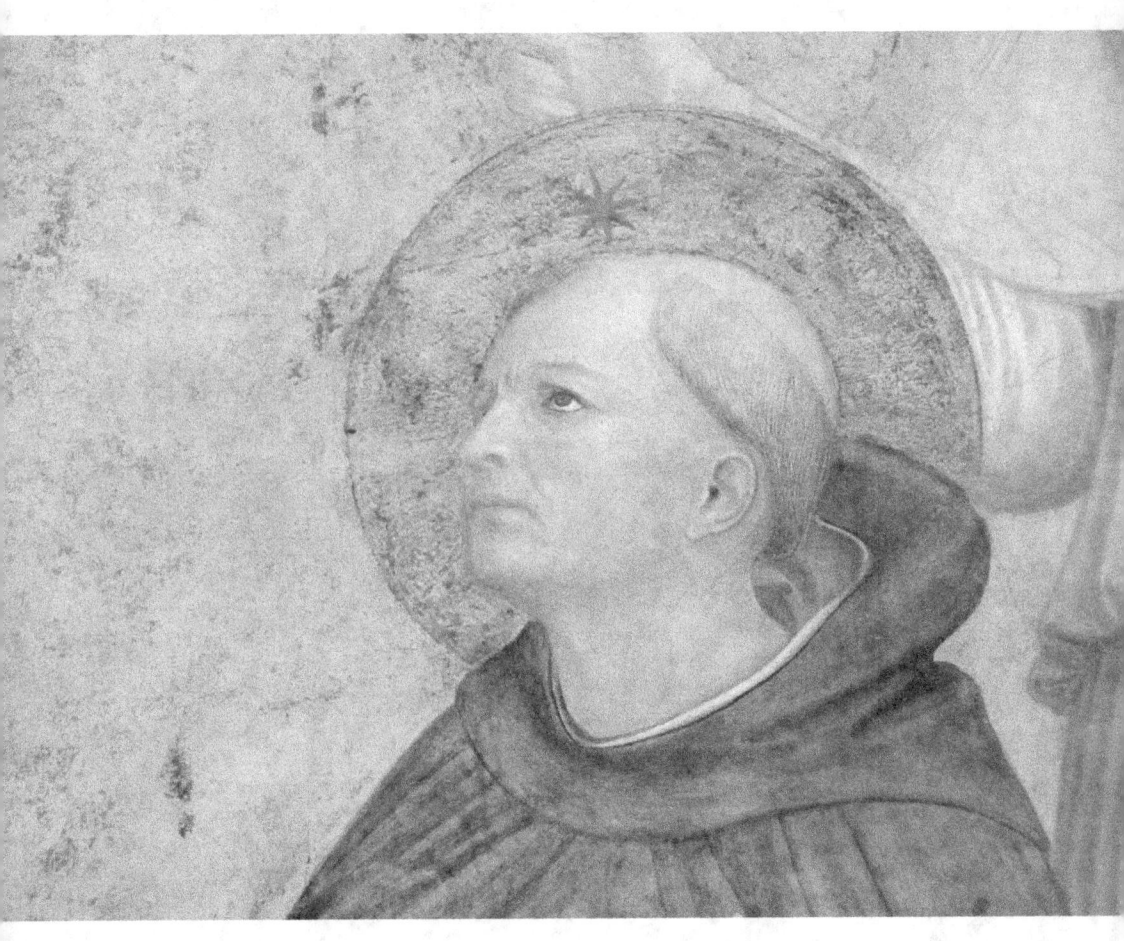

Fra Angelico, Crucifixion, detail, 1441-42, San Marco

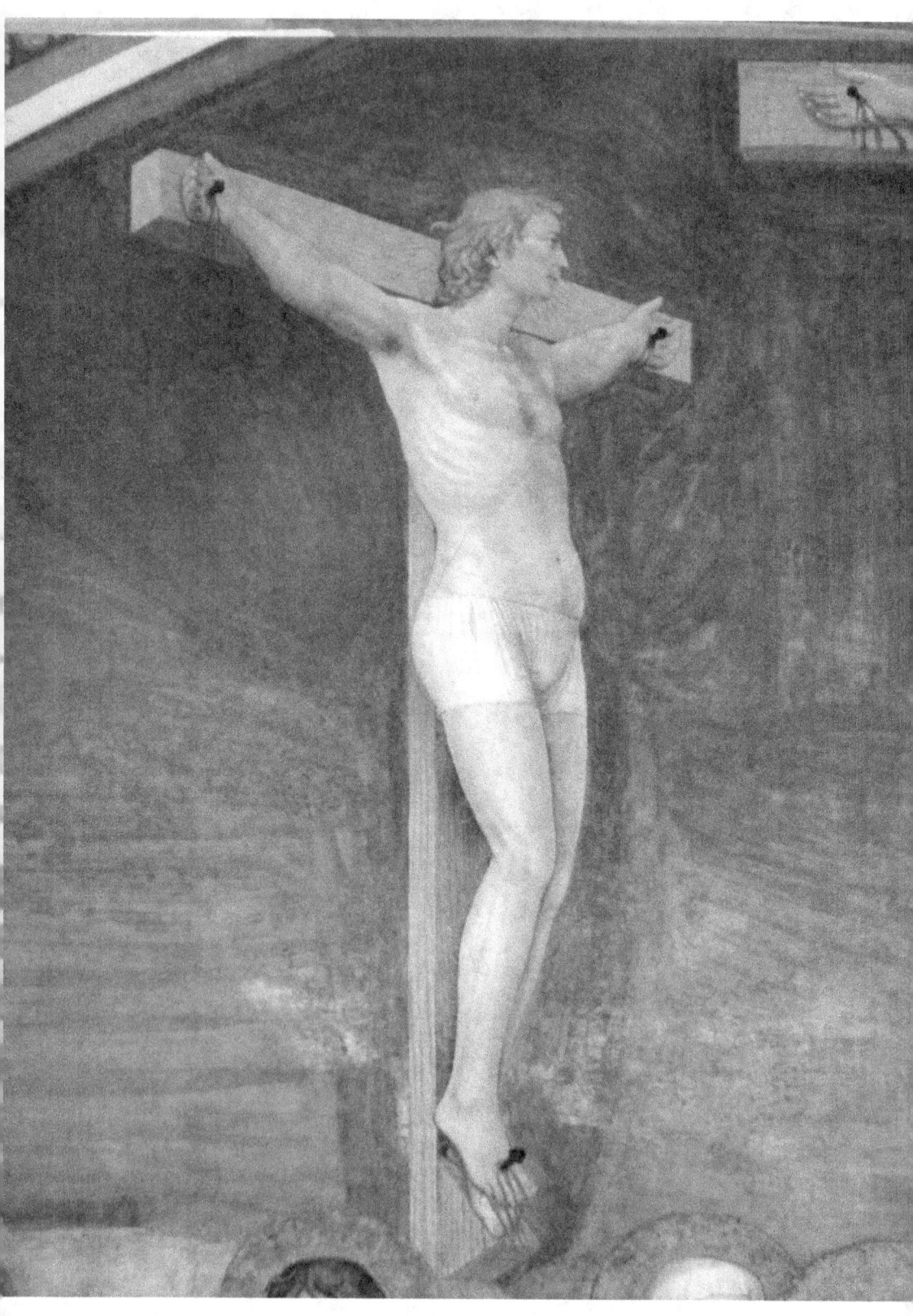

Fra Angelico, Crucifixion, 1441-42, San Marco, detail

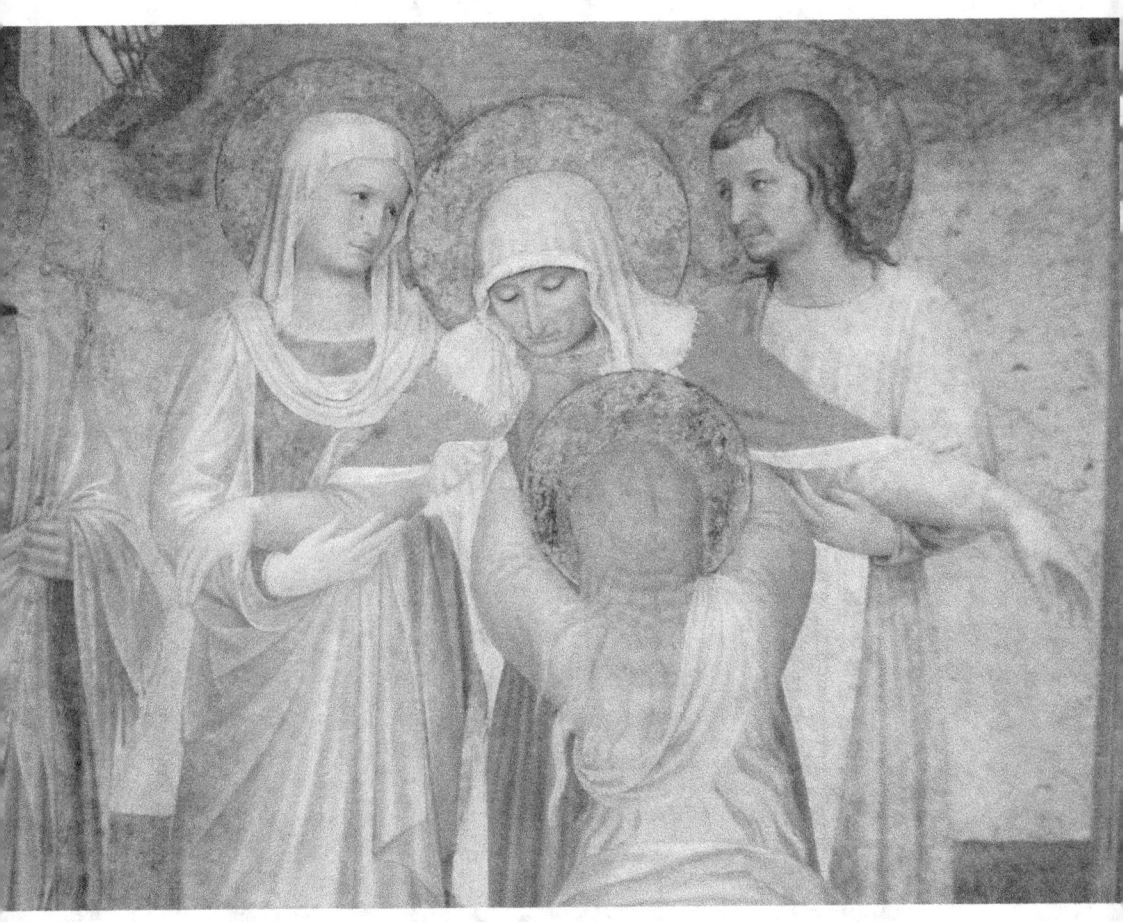

Fra Angelico, Crucifixion, detail

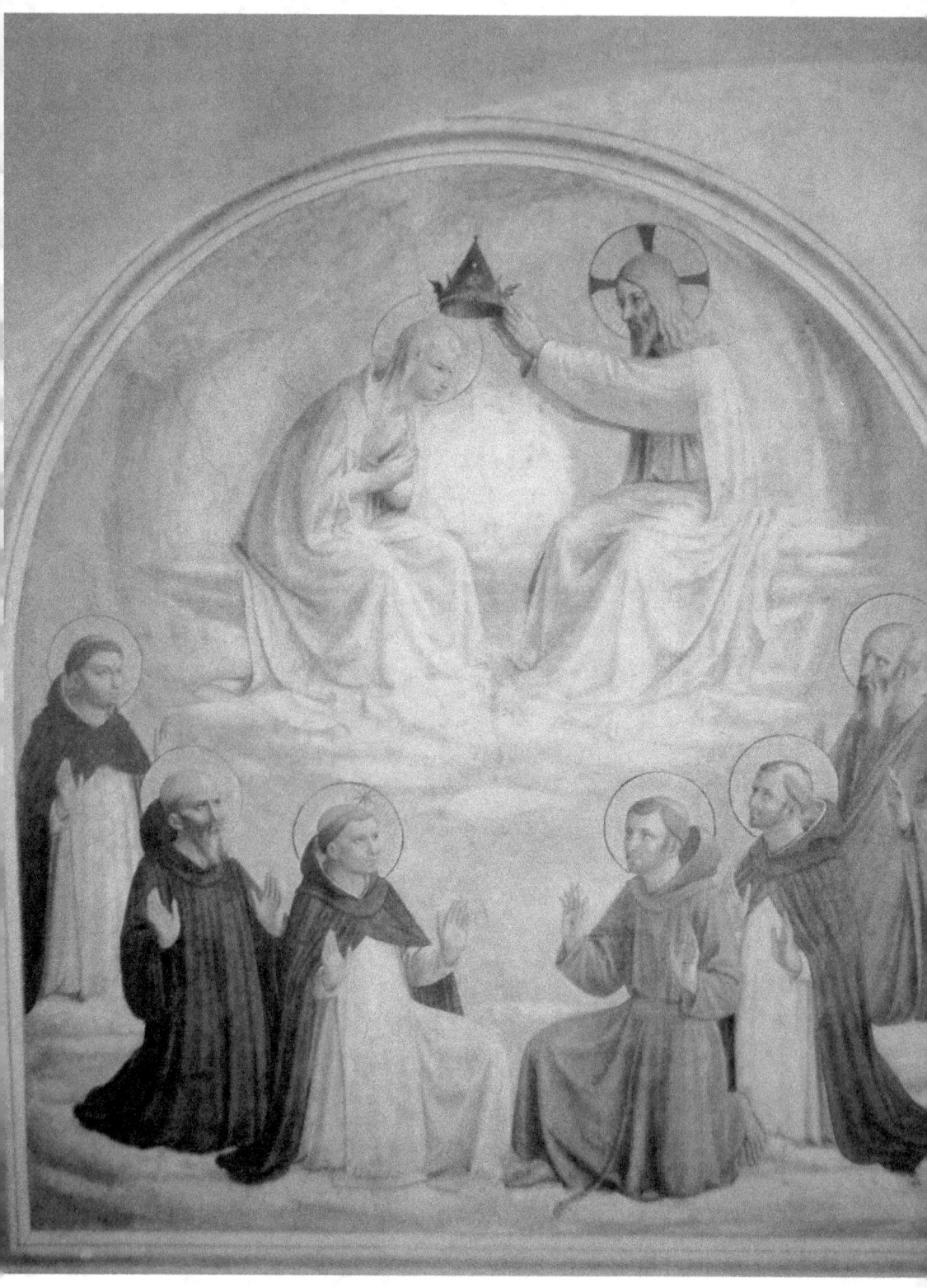

Fra Angelico, The Coronation of the Virgin, San Marco

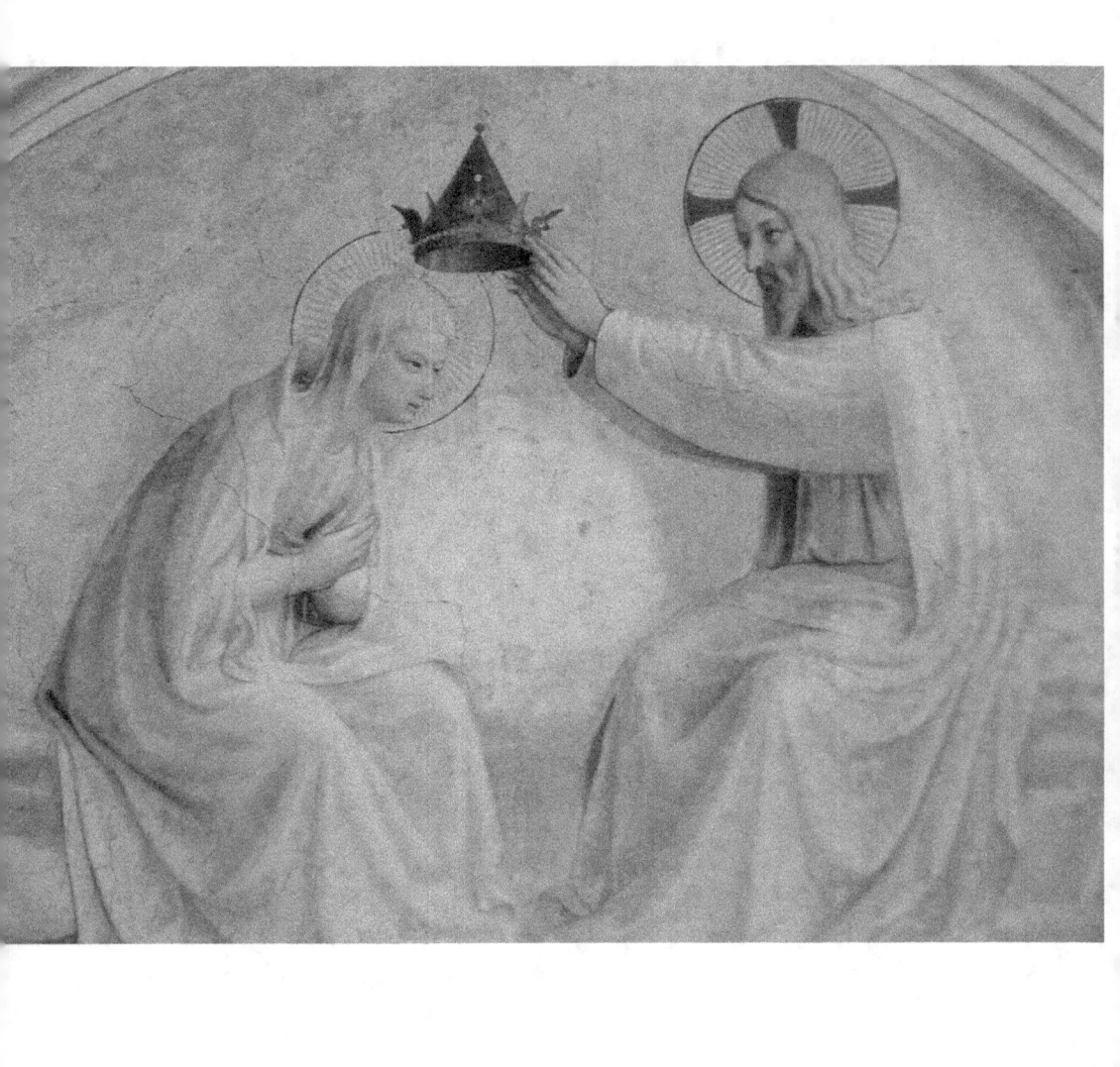

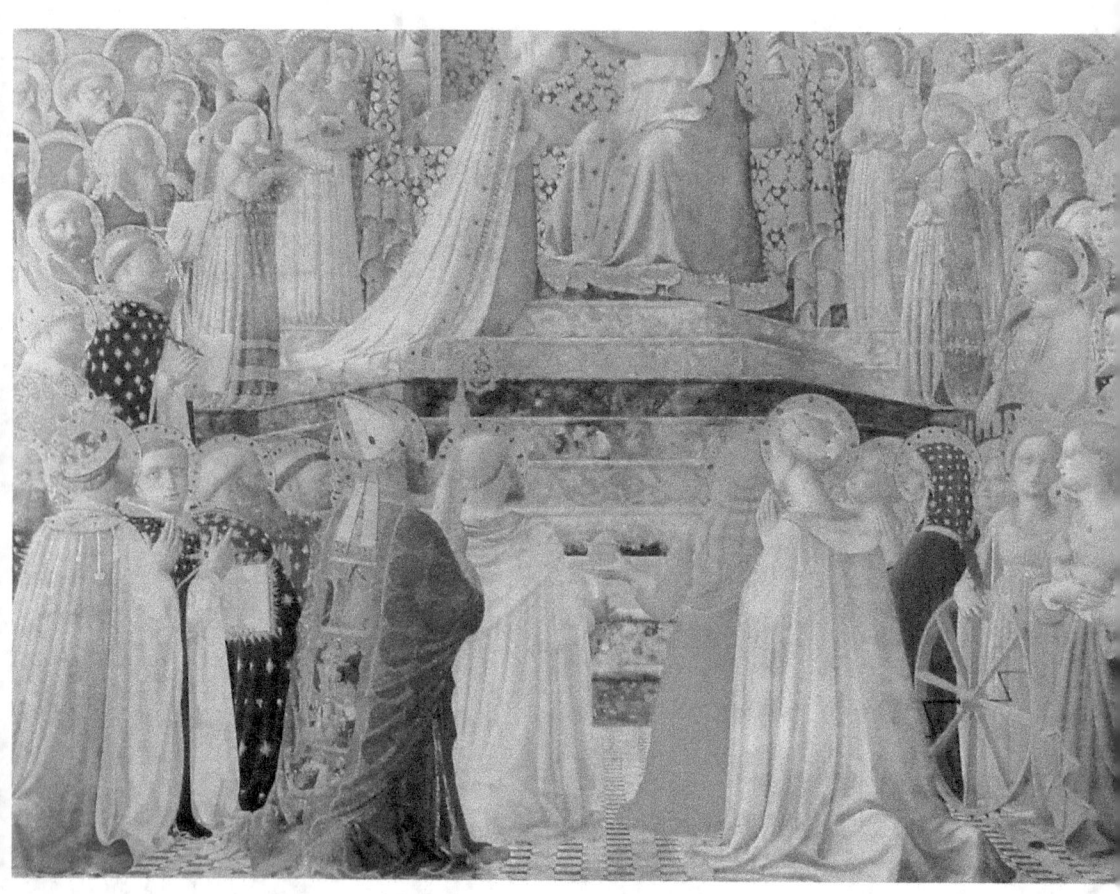

Fra Angelico, The Coronation of the Virgin, Louve, Paris, detail

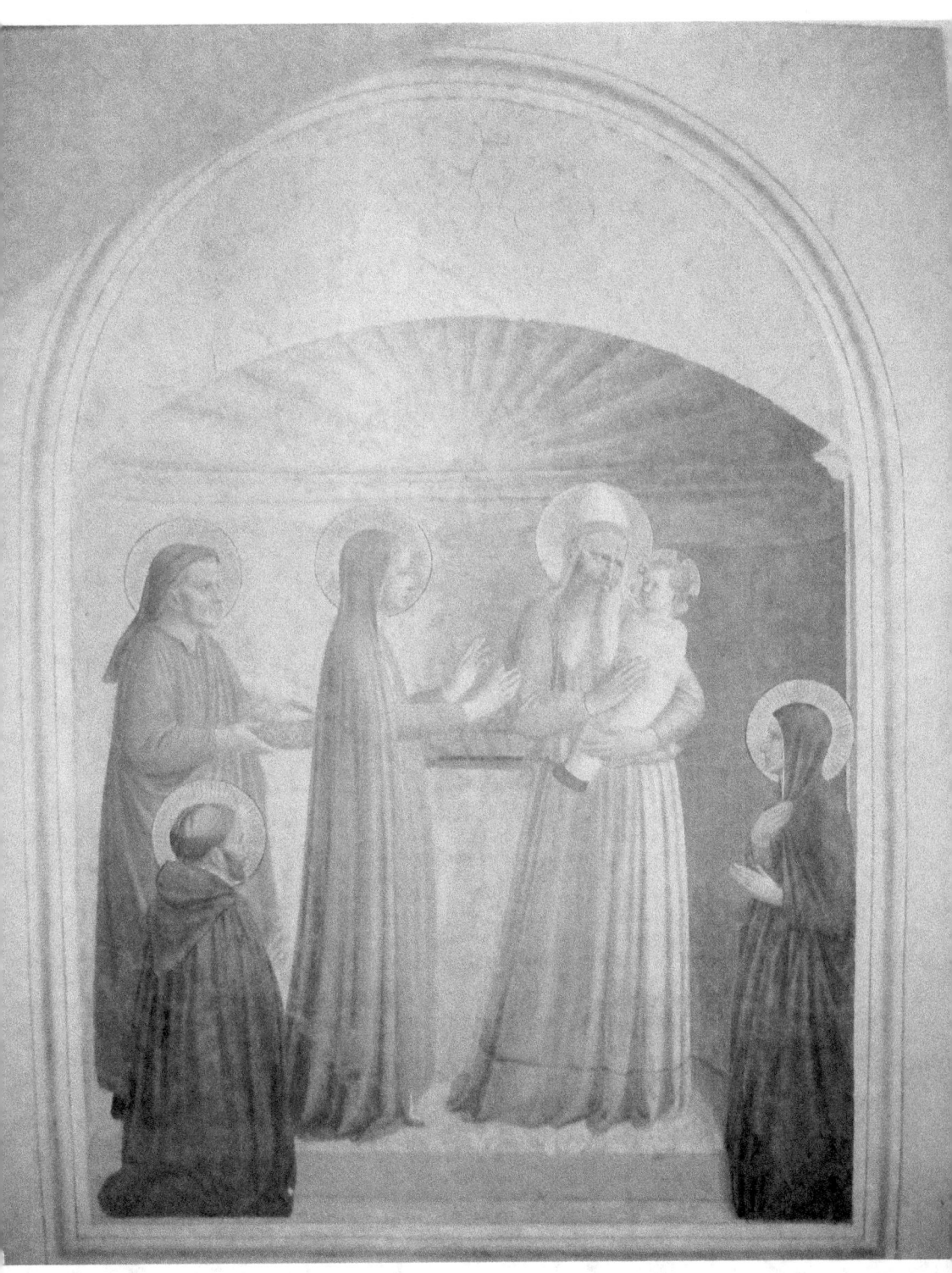

Fra Angelico, Presentation In the Temple, San Marco

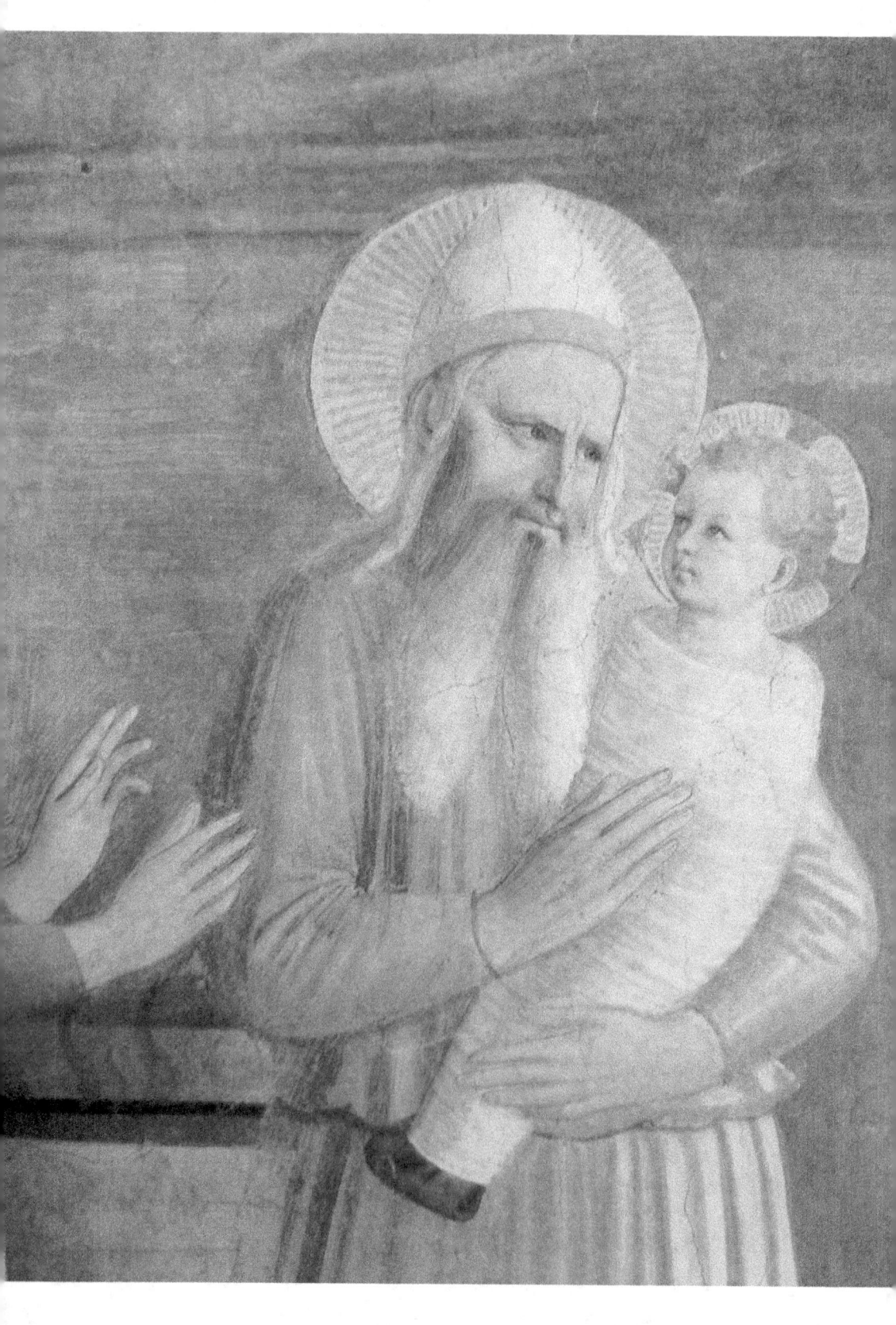

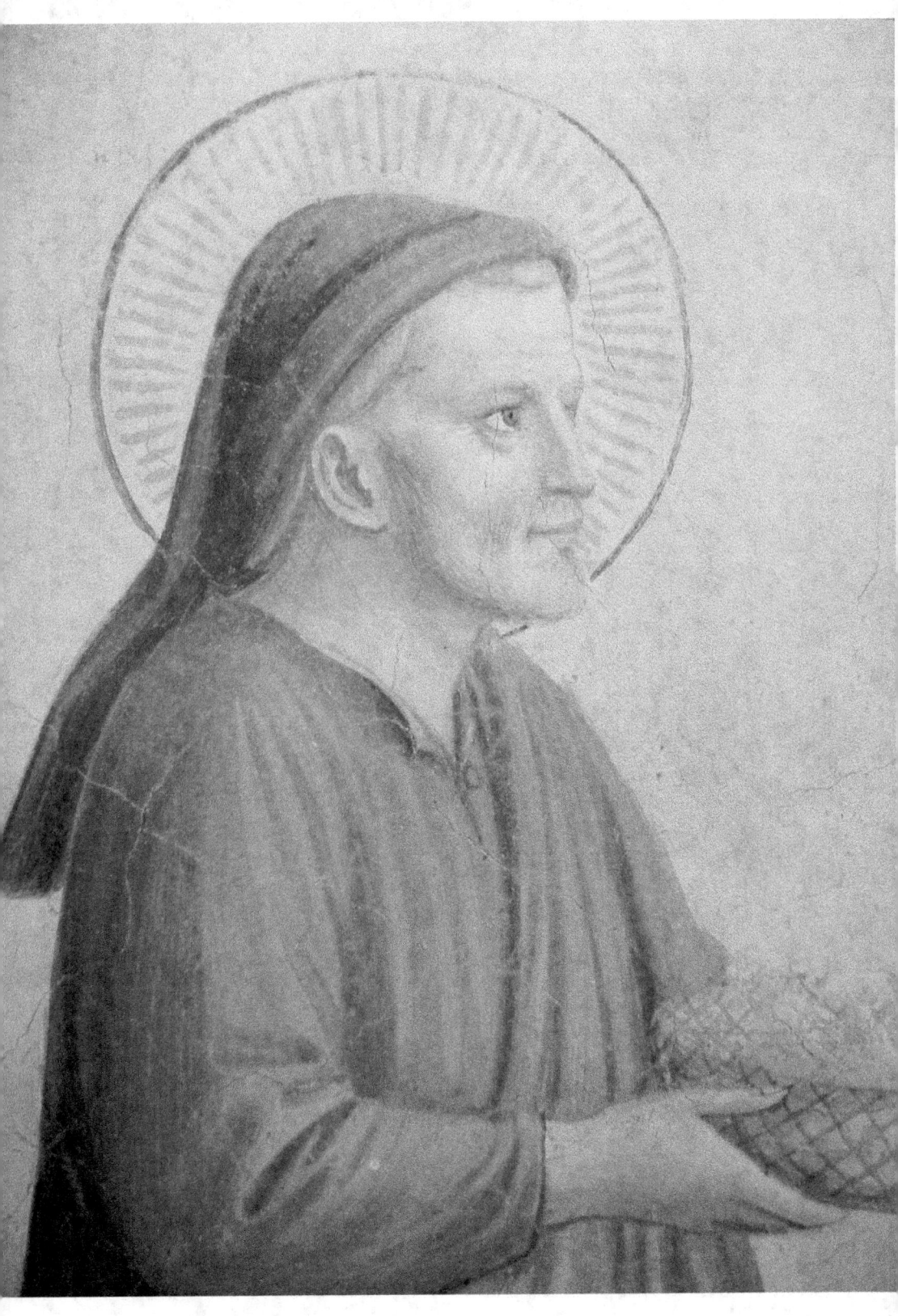

Fra Angelico, Presentation In the Temple, 1440-41, San Marco

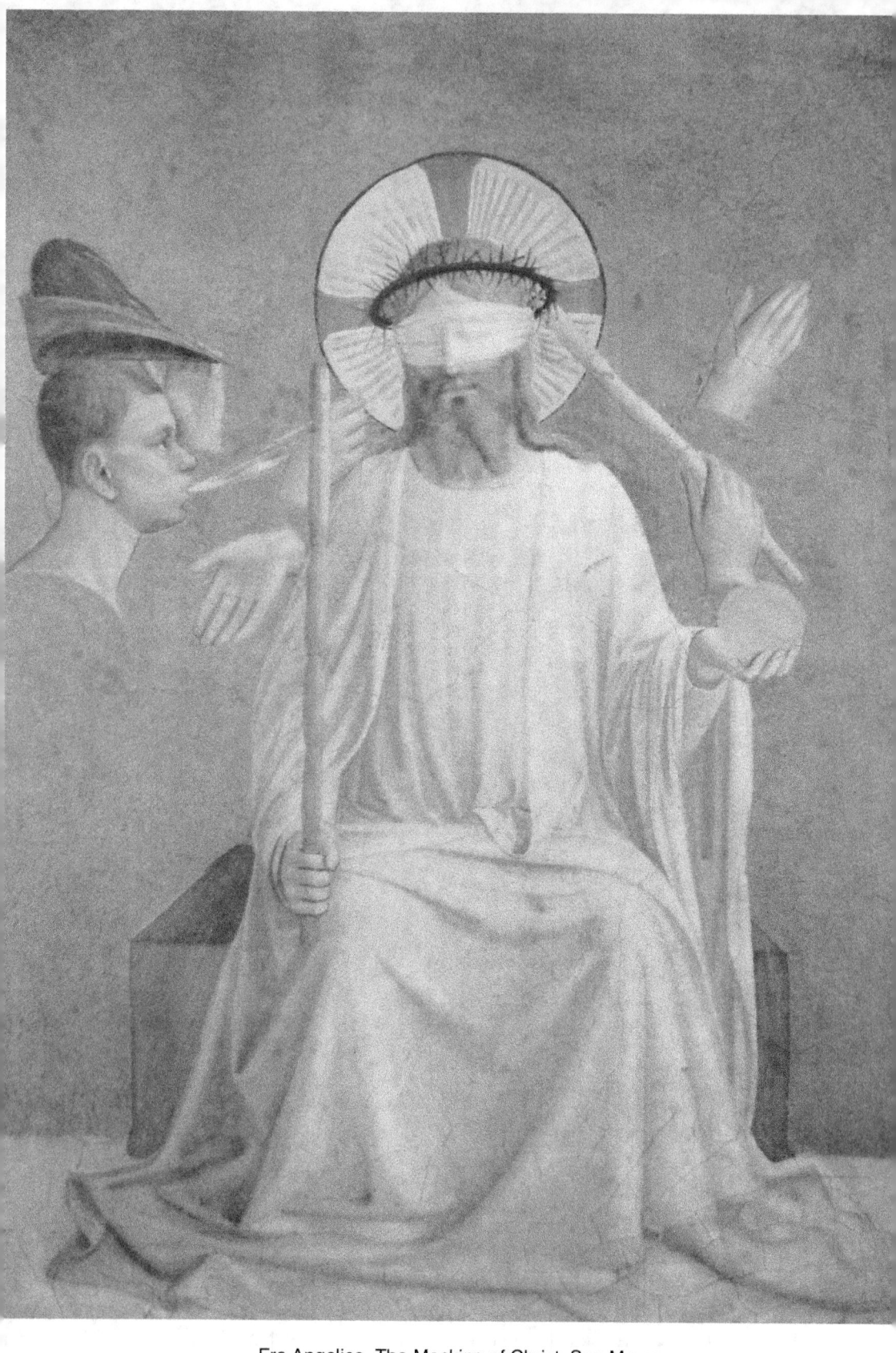

Fra Angelico, The Mocking of Christ, San Marco

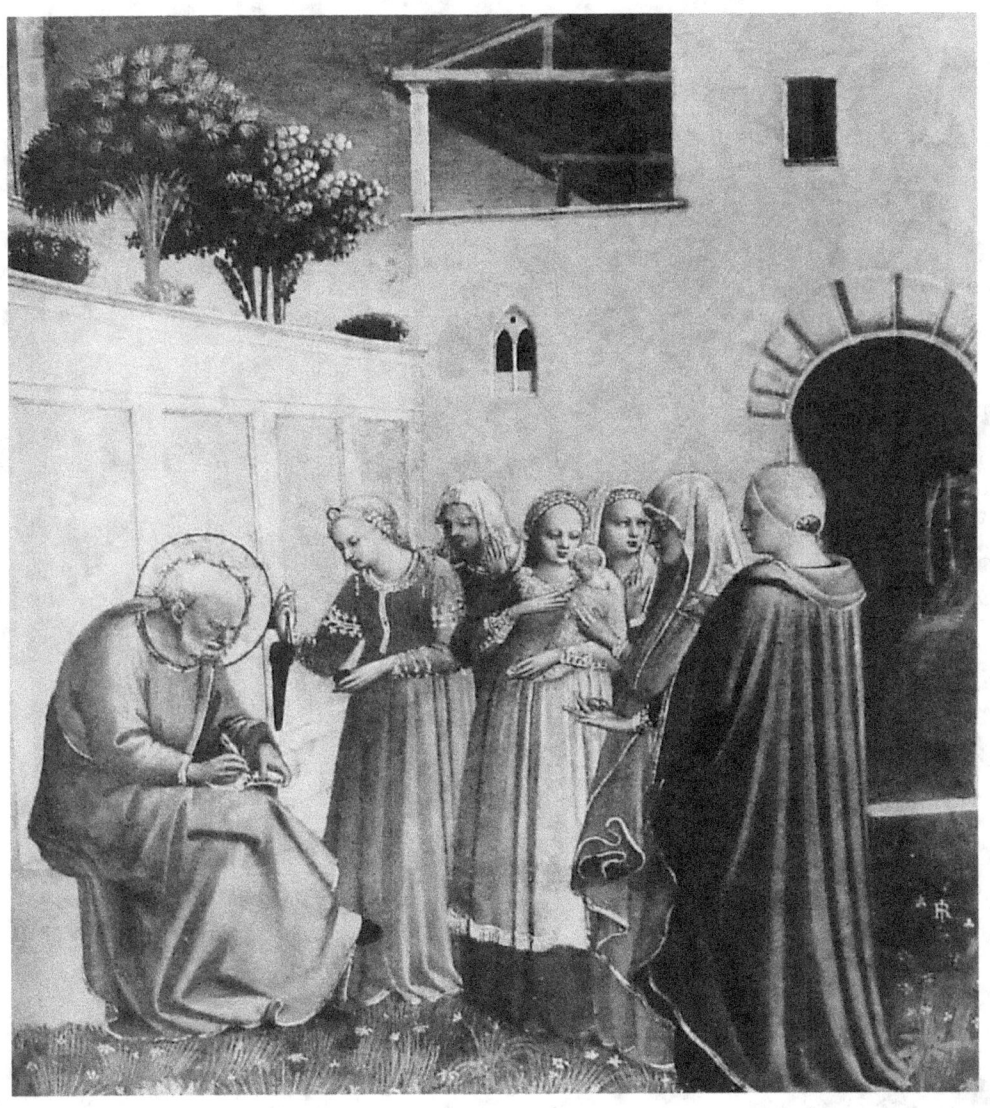

Fra Angelico, The Naming of John the Baptist, 1435

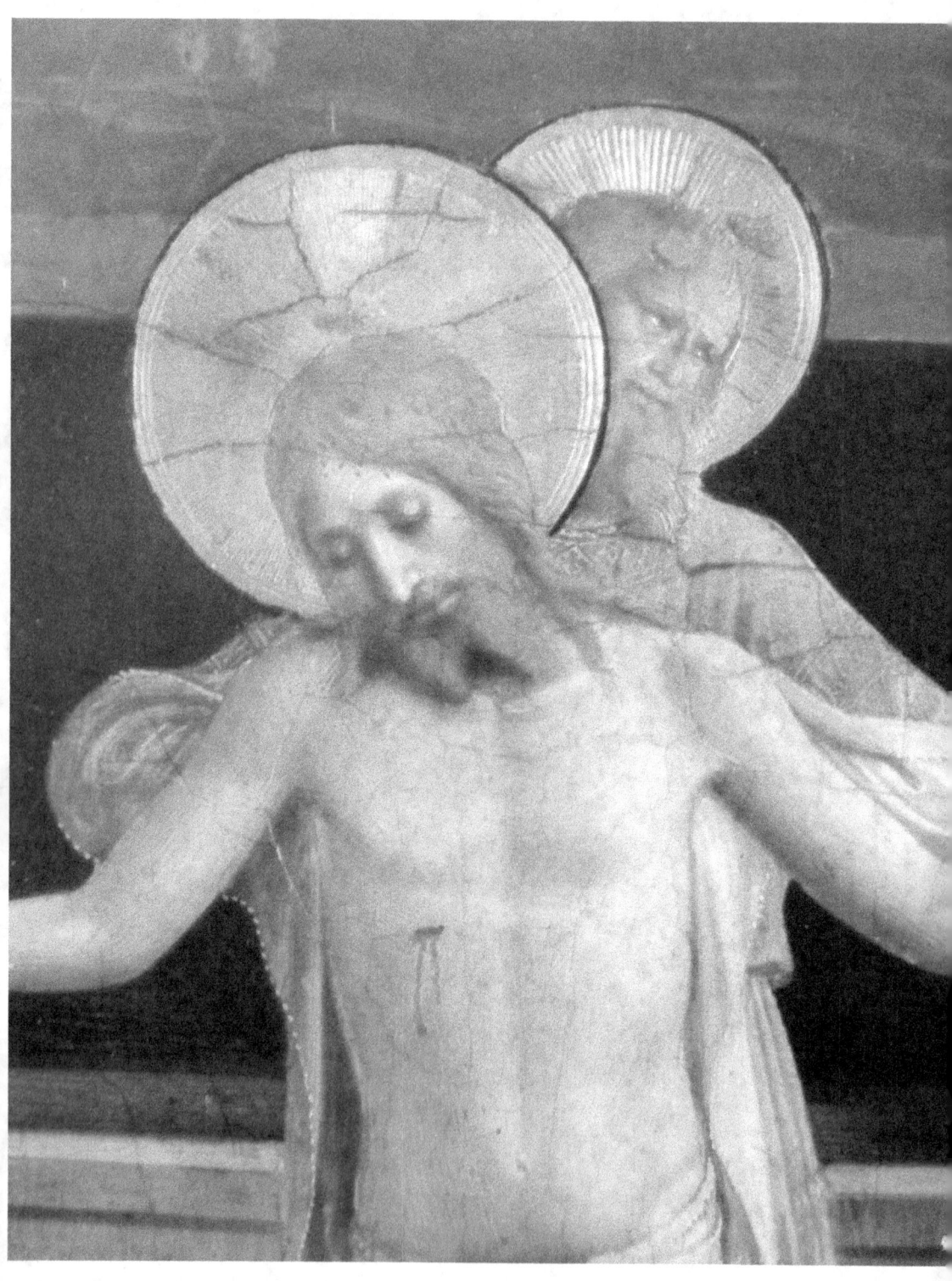

Fra Angelico, Lamentation Over the Dead Christ,
Alte Pinakothek, Munich, detail

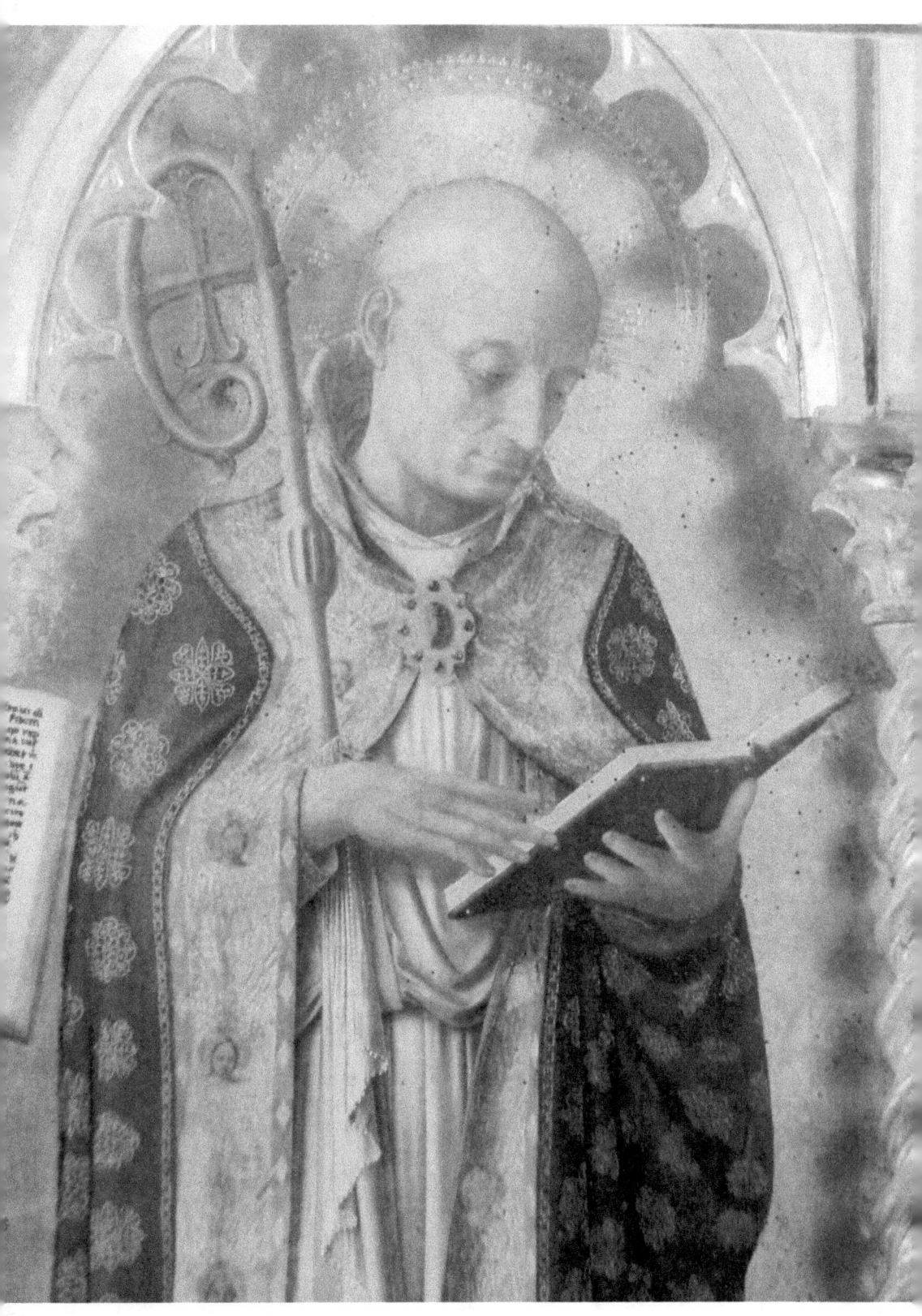

Fra Angelico, Perugia Altarpiece, 1448, detail

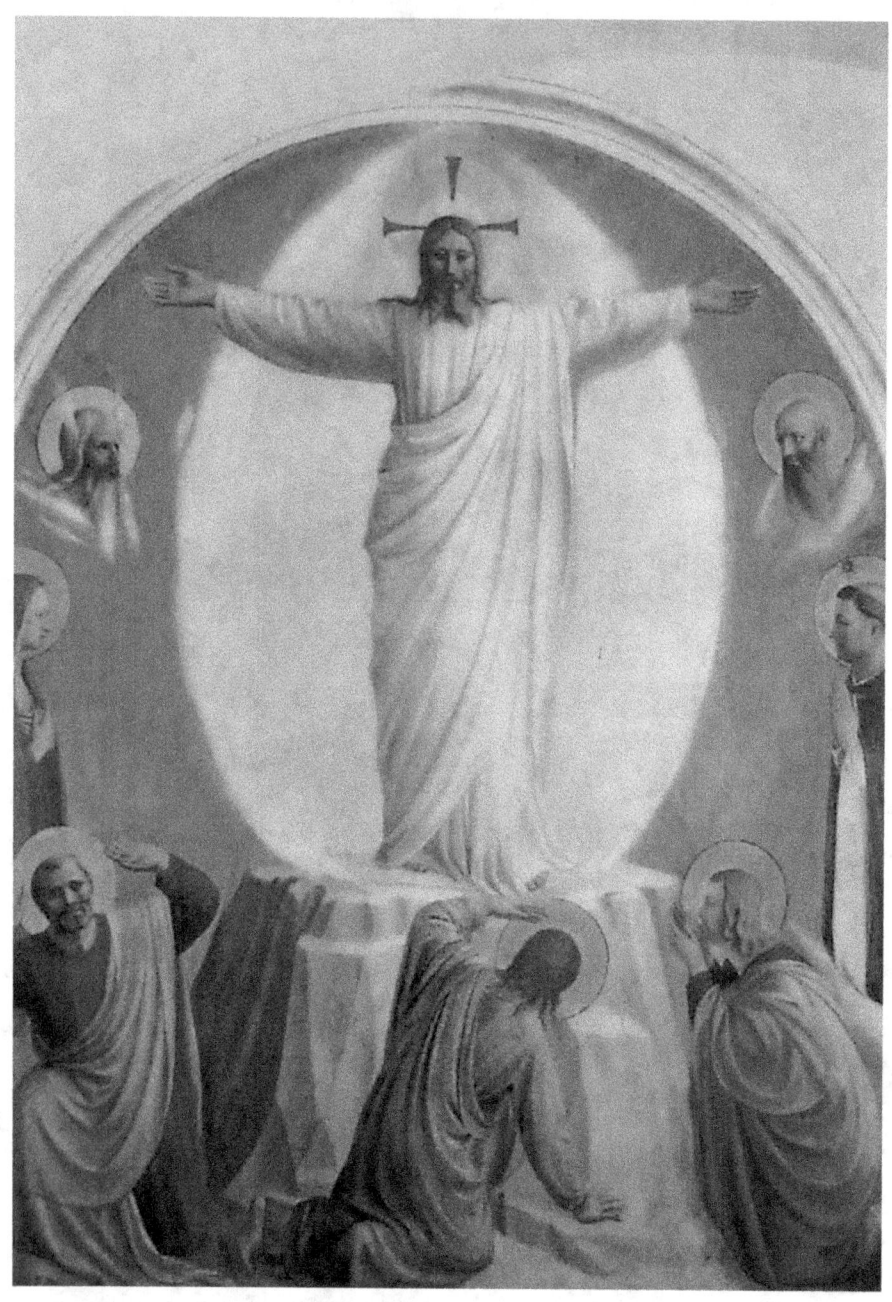

Fra Angelico, The Resurrection, San Marco, Florence

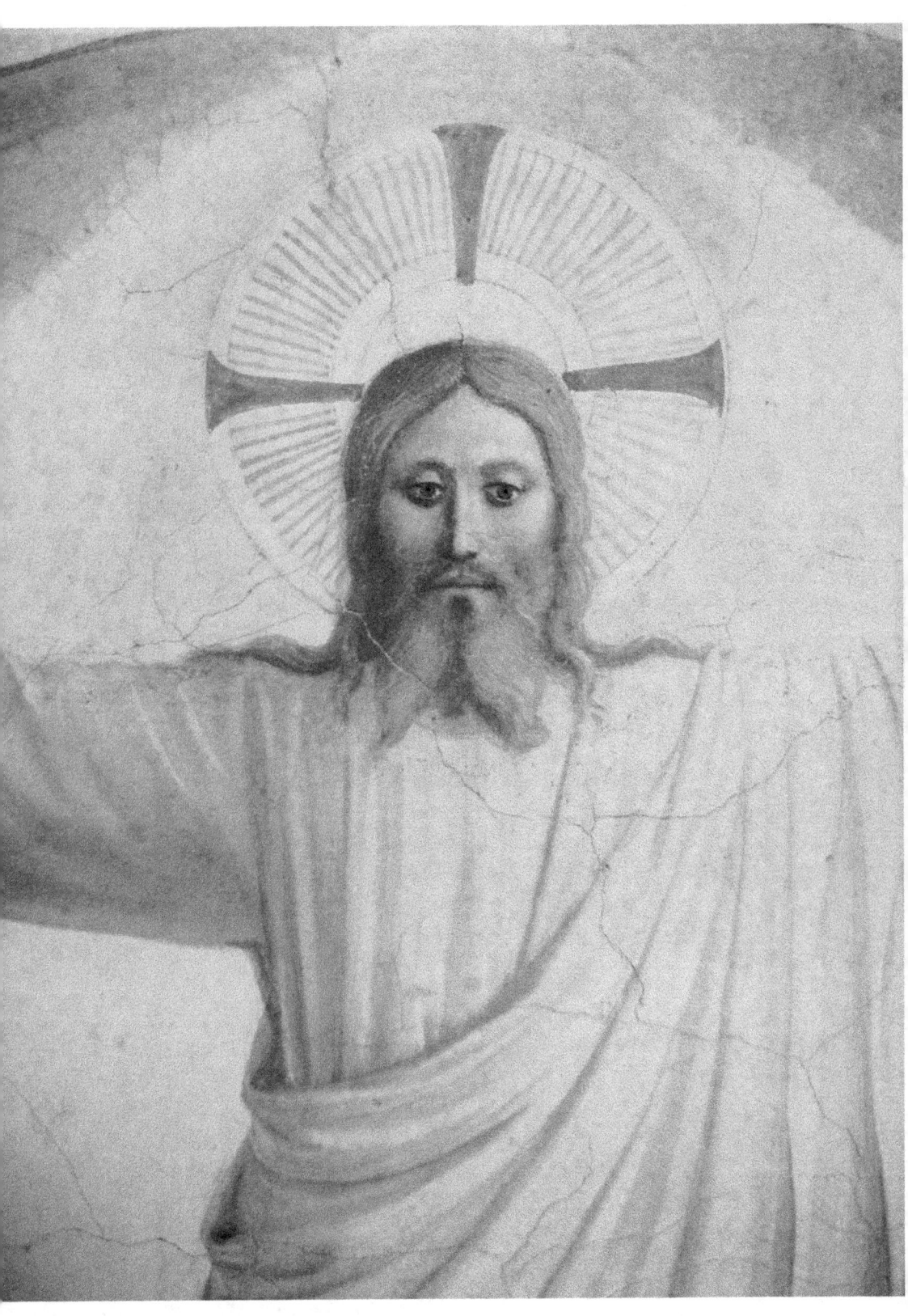

Fra Angelico, The Transfiguration, 1440-41, San Marco, detail

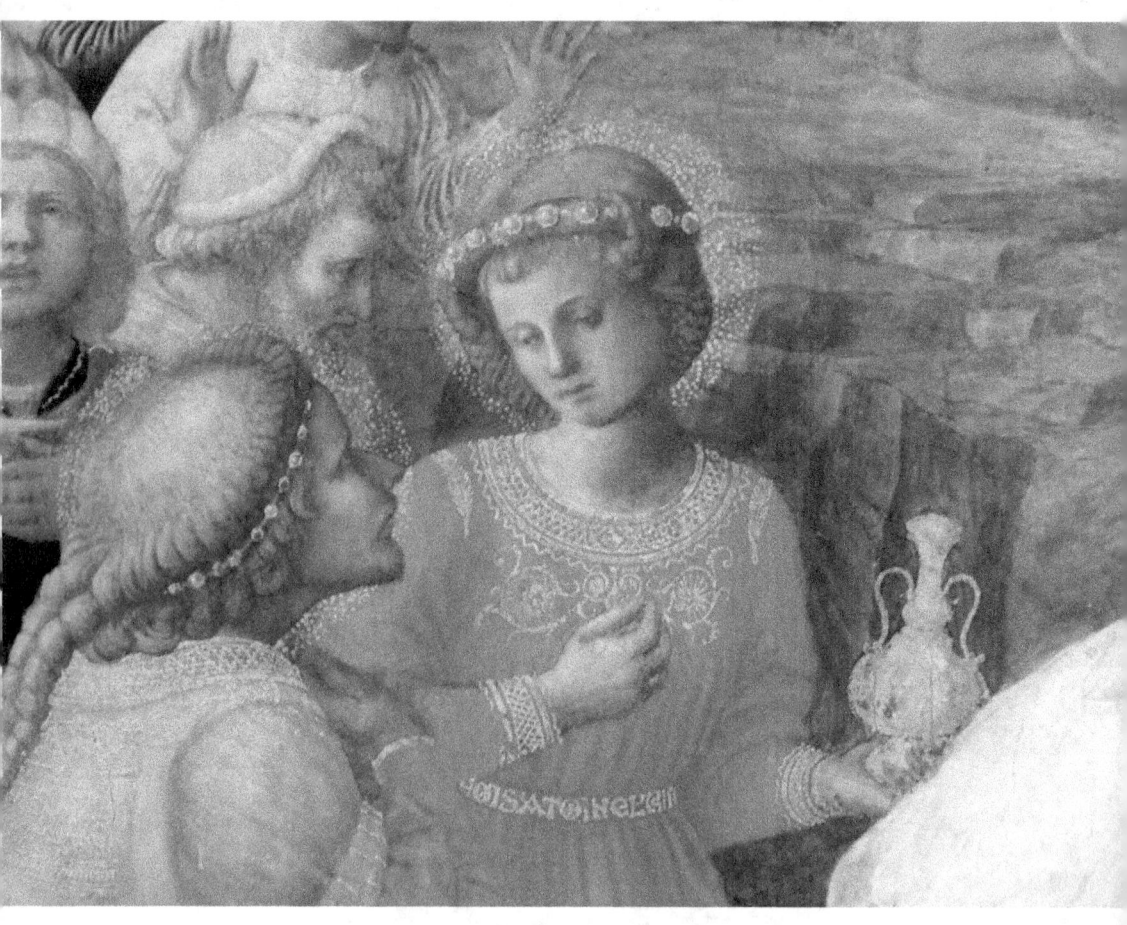

Fra Angelico, detail of Adoration of the Magi, 1445,
National Gallery of Art, Washington, DC (photo: author)

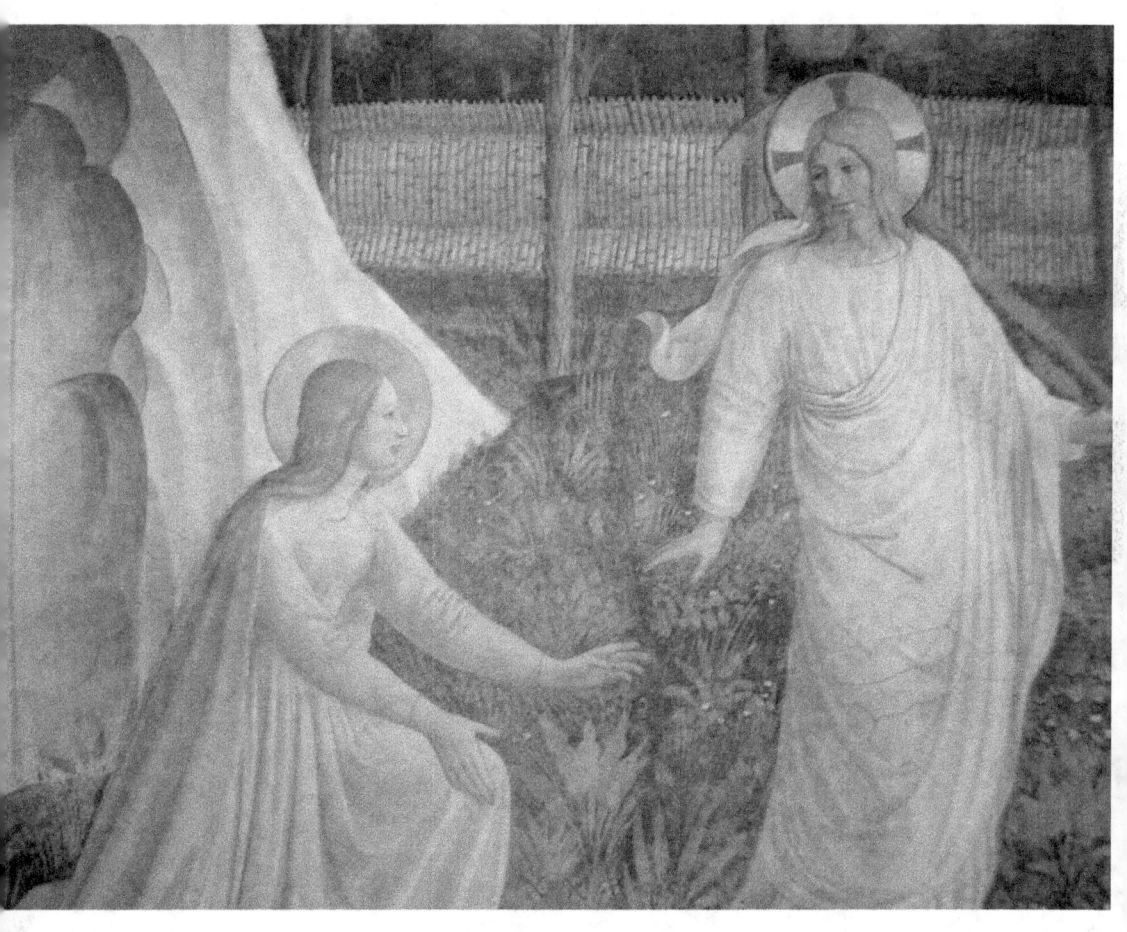

Fra Angelico, Noli Me Tangere

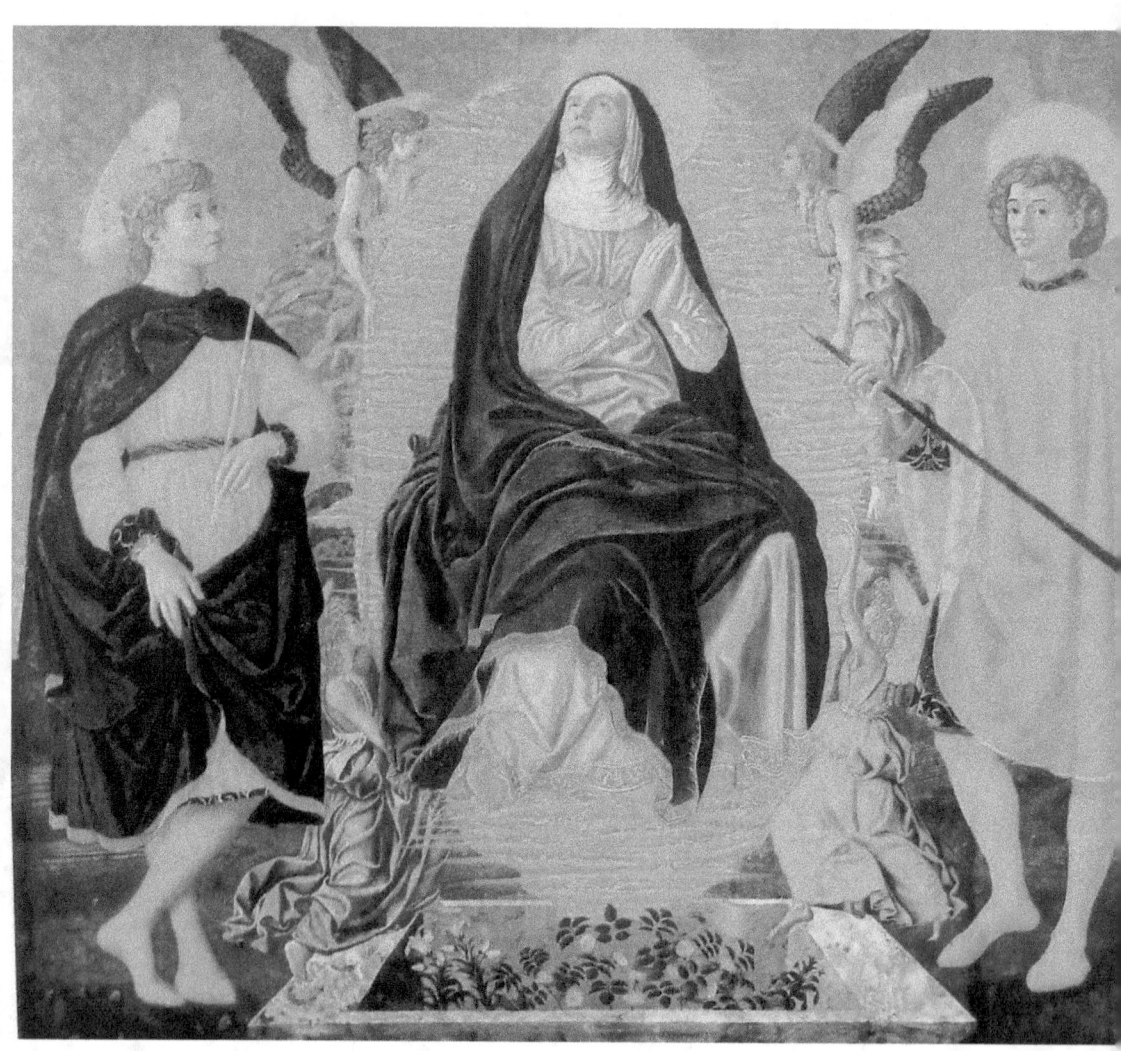

Andrea del Castagno, Assumption, Berlin

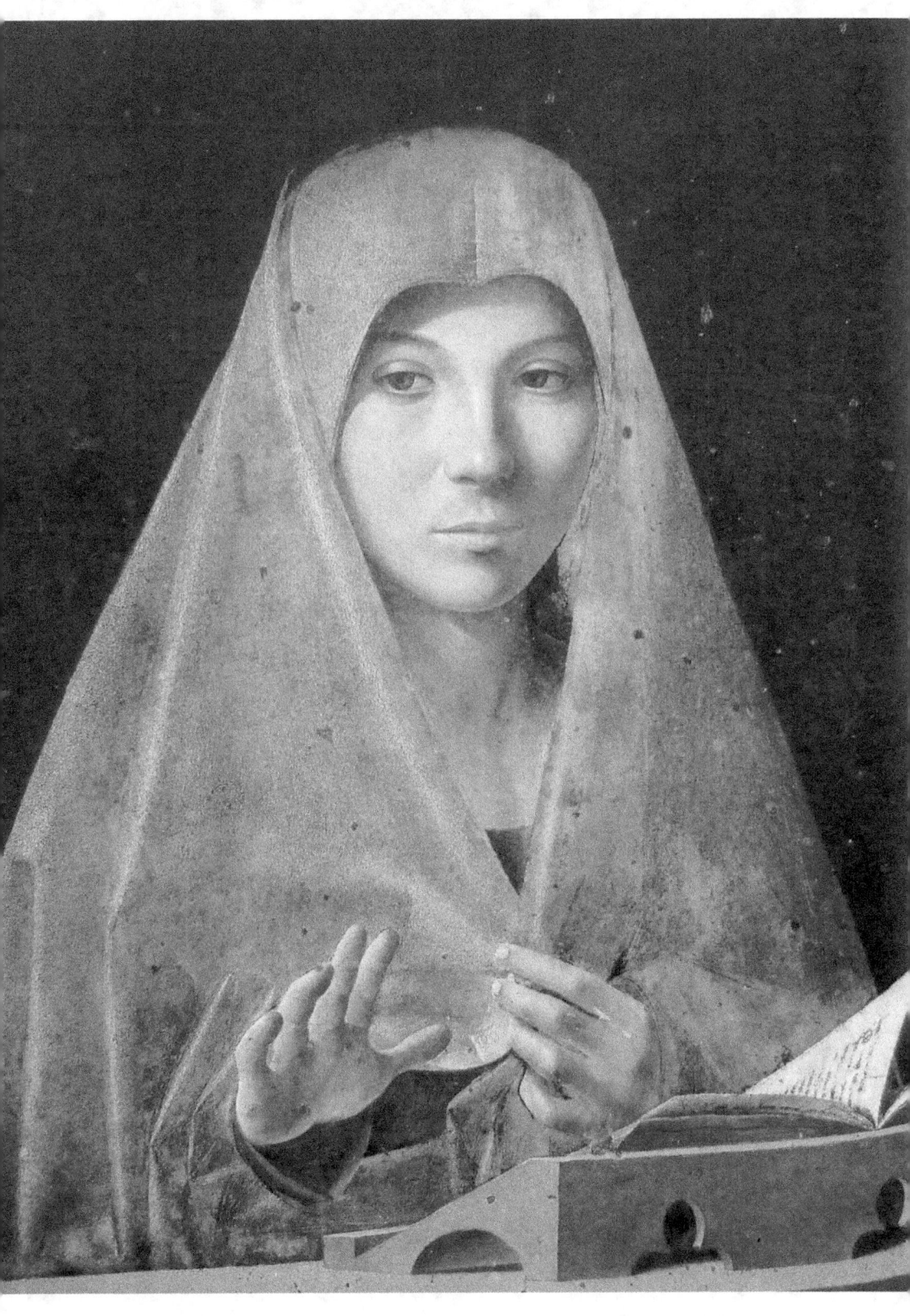

Antonello da Messina, The Virgin of the Annunciation, 1475, Palermo

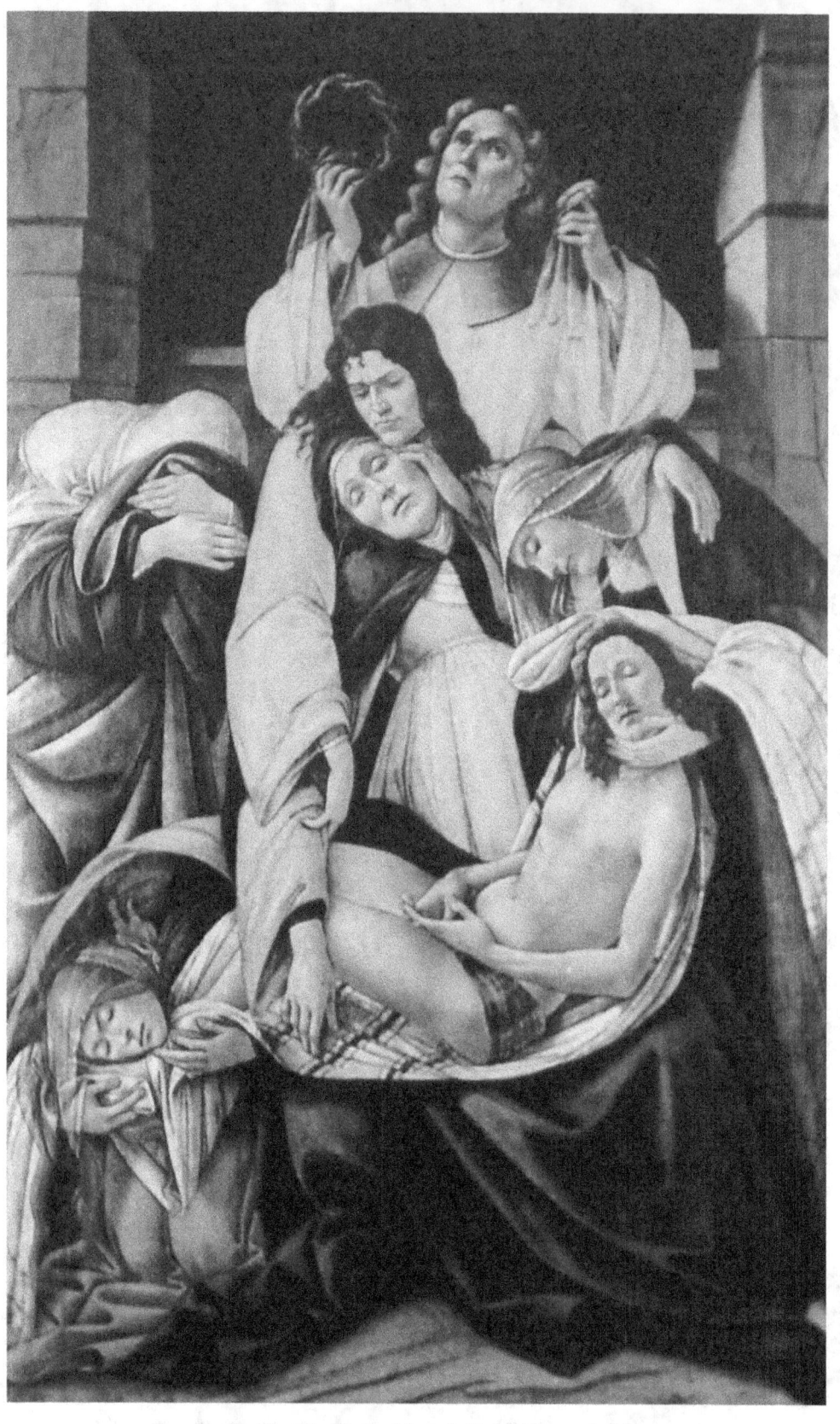

Sandro Botticelli, *Pietà*, Museo Poldi Pezzoli, Milan

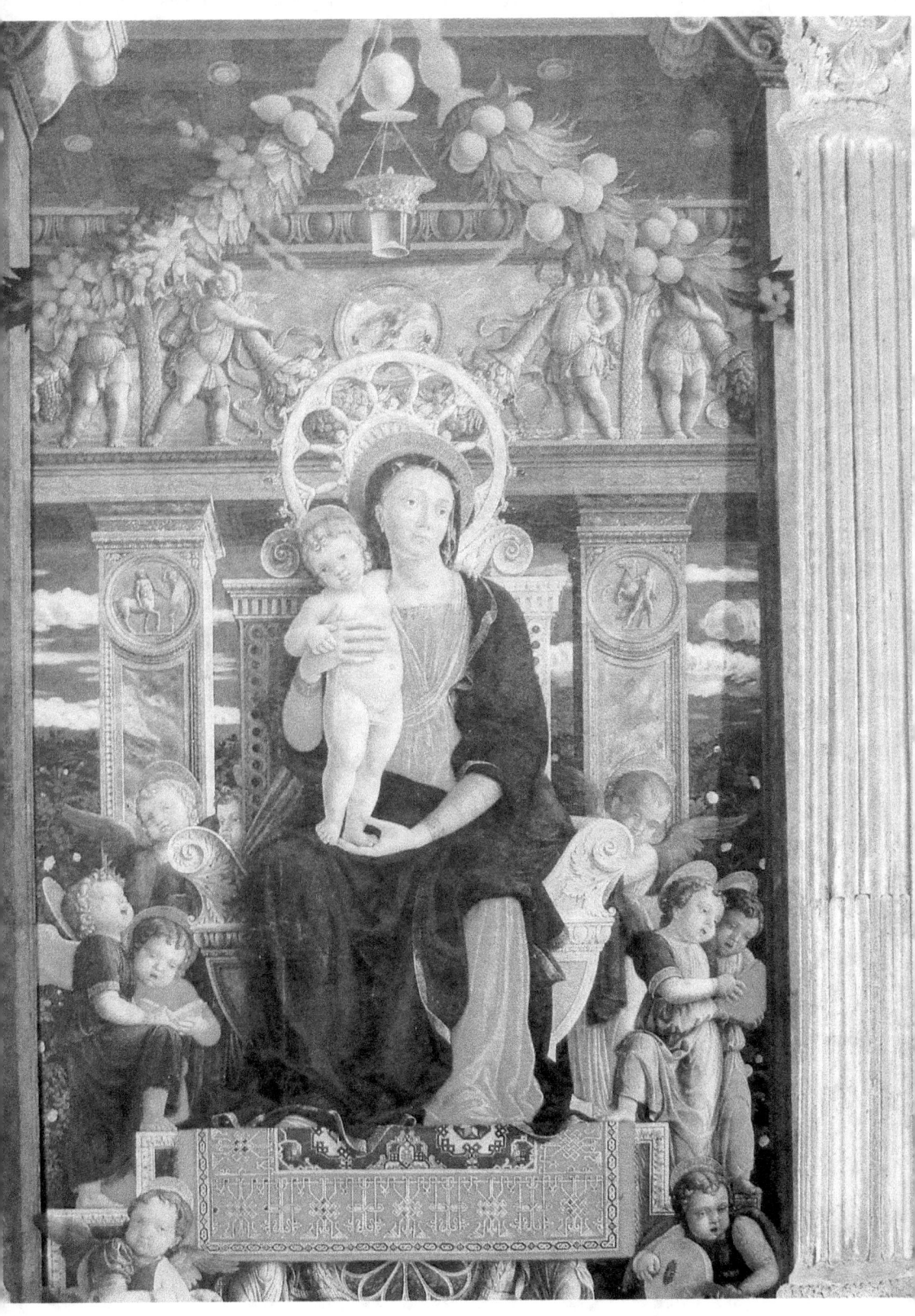

Andreas Mantegna, Madonna and Child Enthroned, 1457-60, Verona

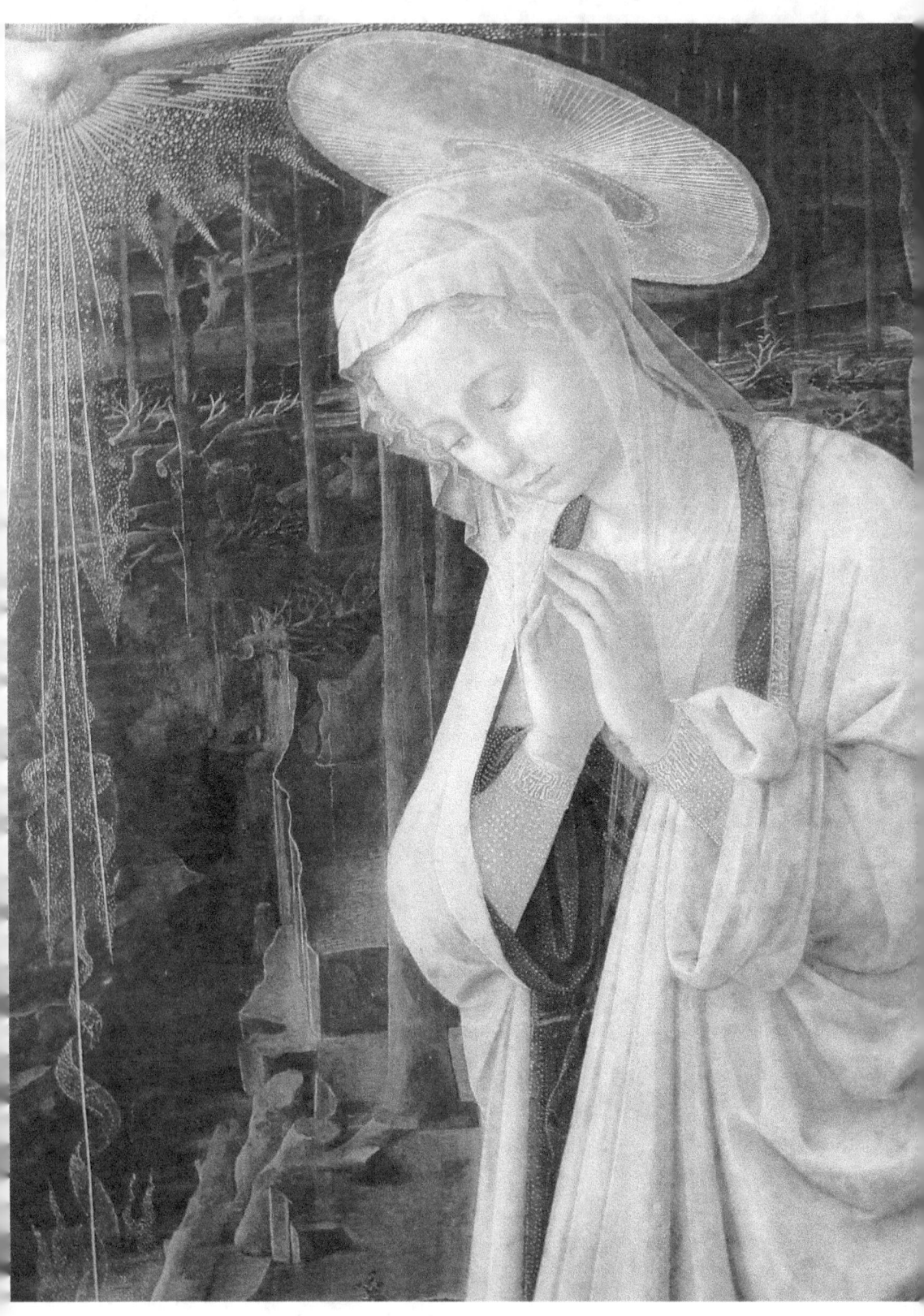

Fra Filippo Lippi, The Adoration of the Virgin, Berlin, detail

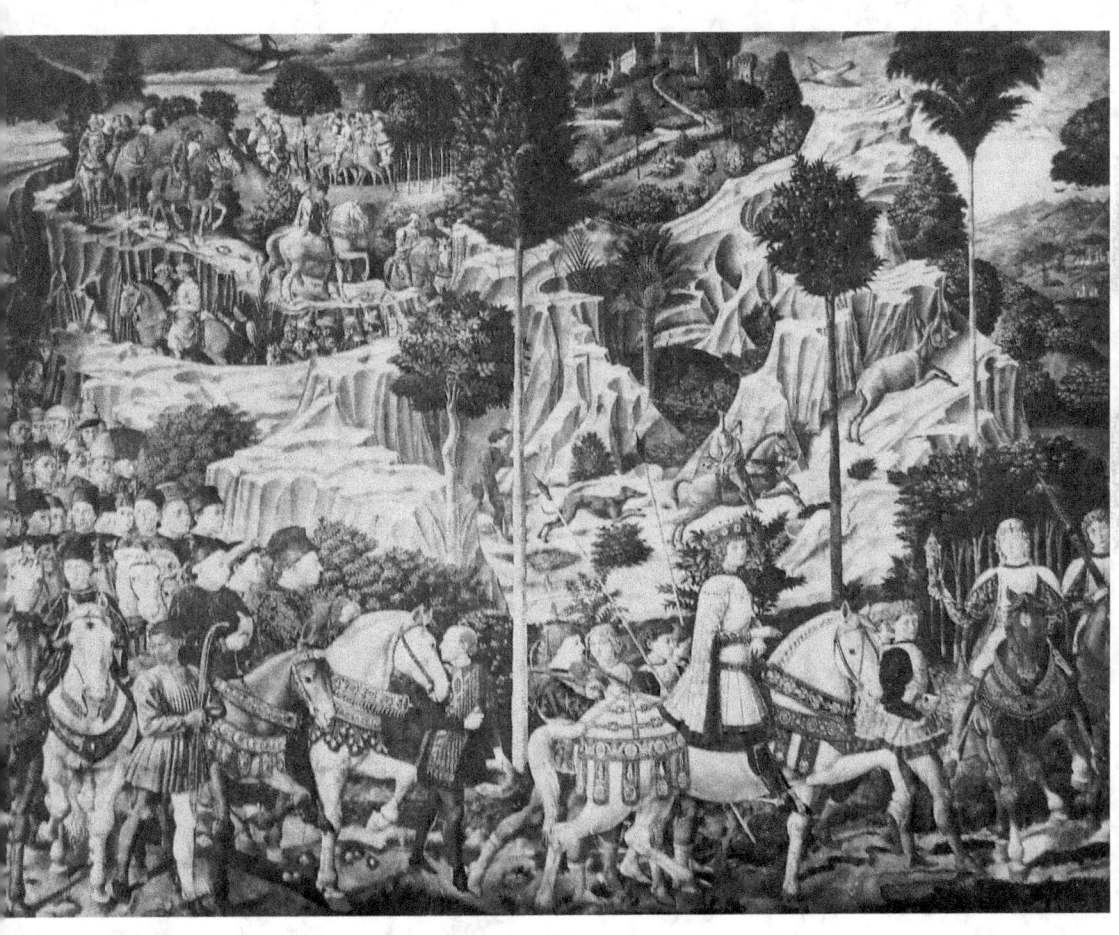

Benozzo Gozzoli, Journey of the Magi

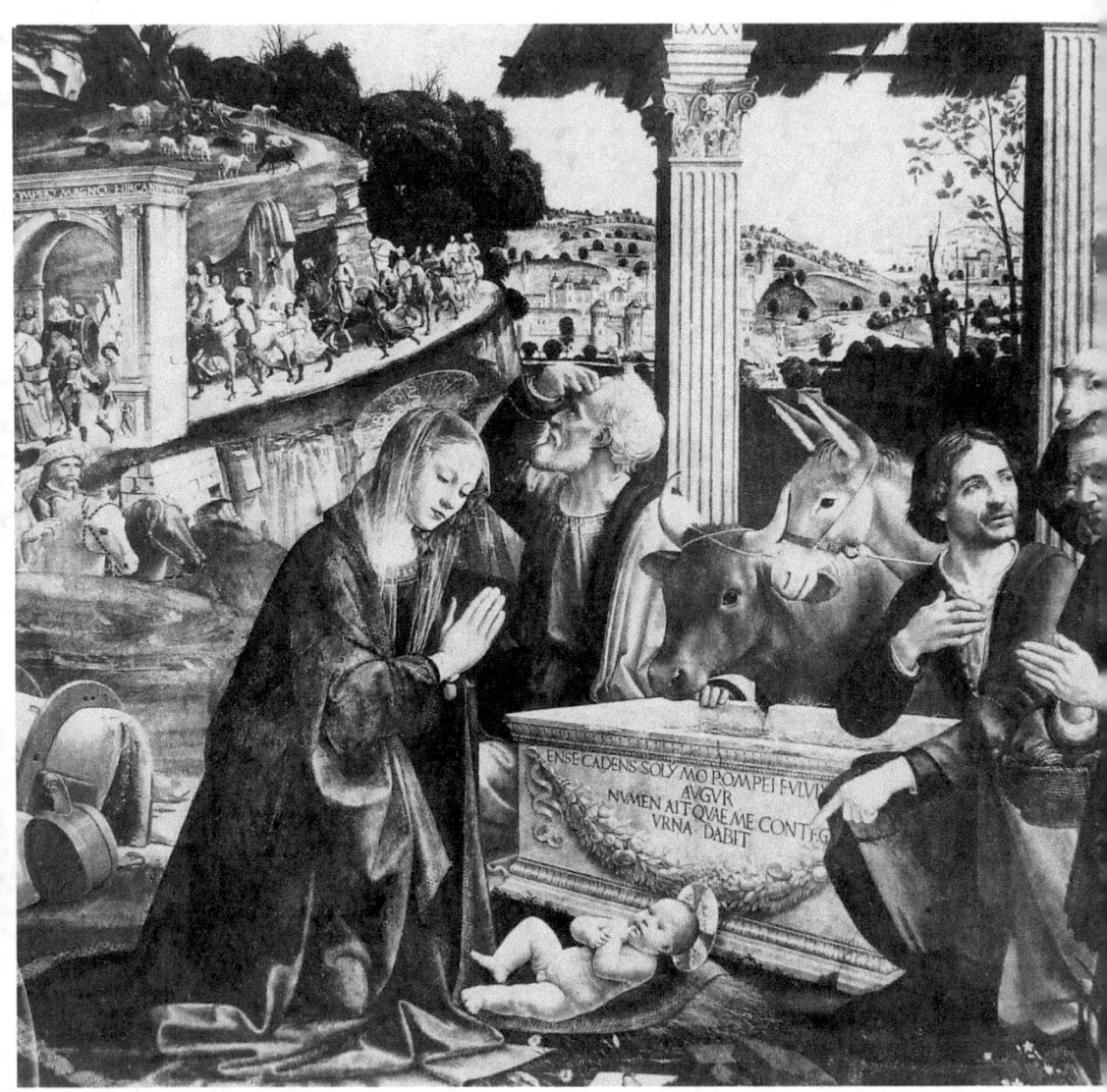

Domenico Ghirlandaio, Adoration of the Shepherds, 1485

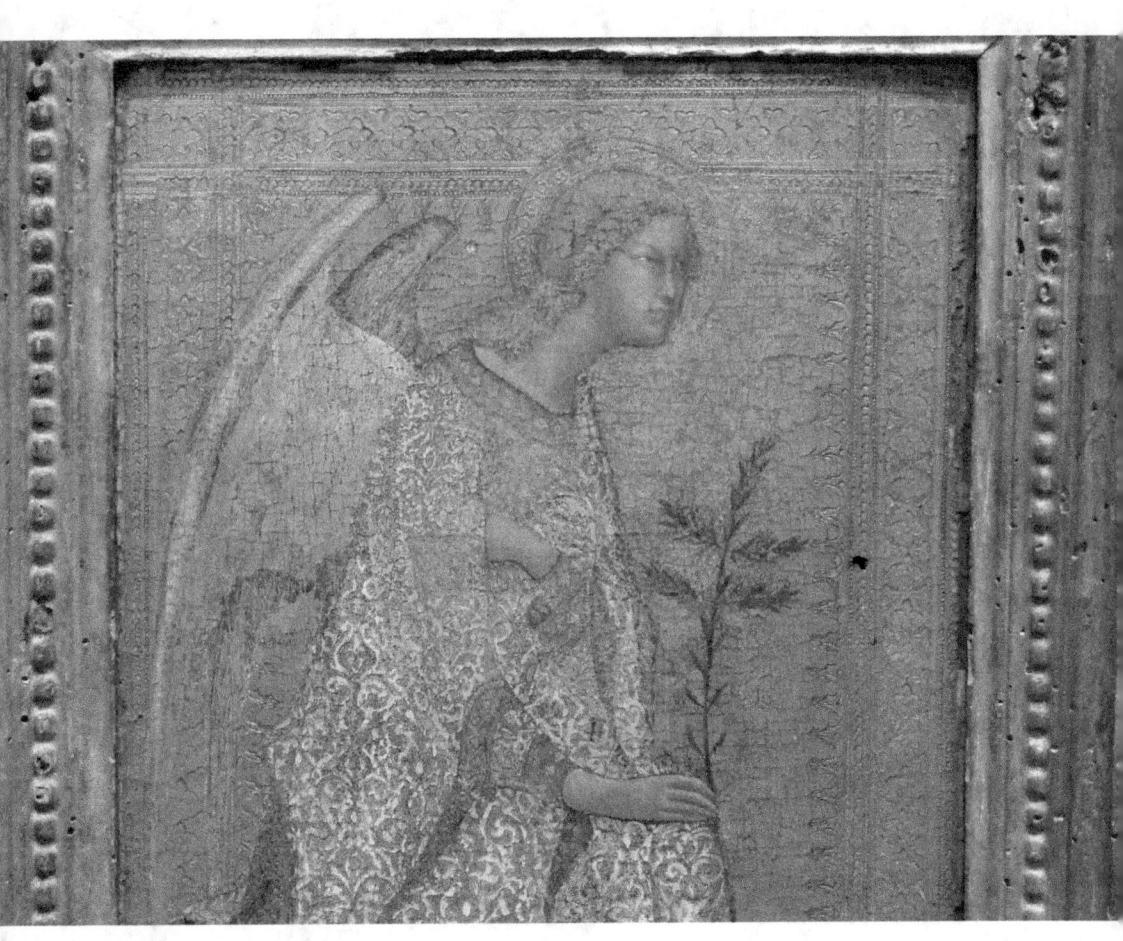

Simone Martini, Annunciation, Metropolitan Museum of Art, New York

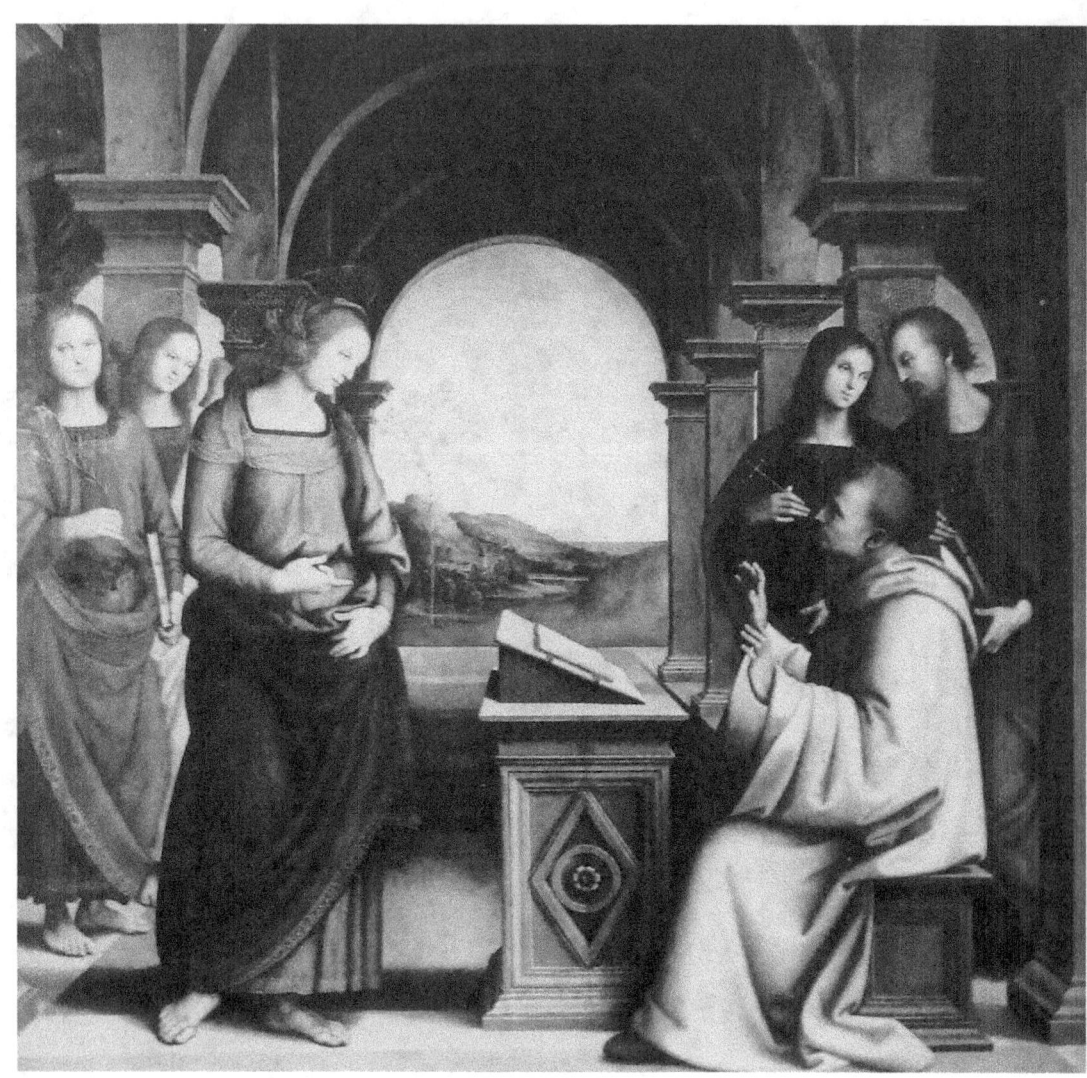

Perugino, Vision of St Bernard, 1488

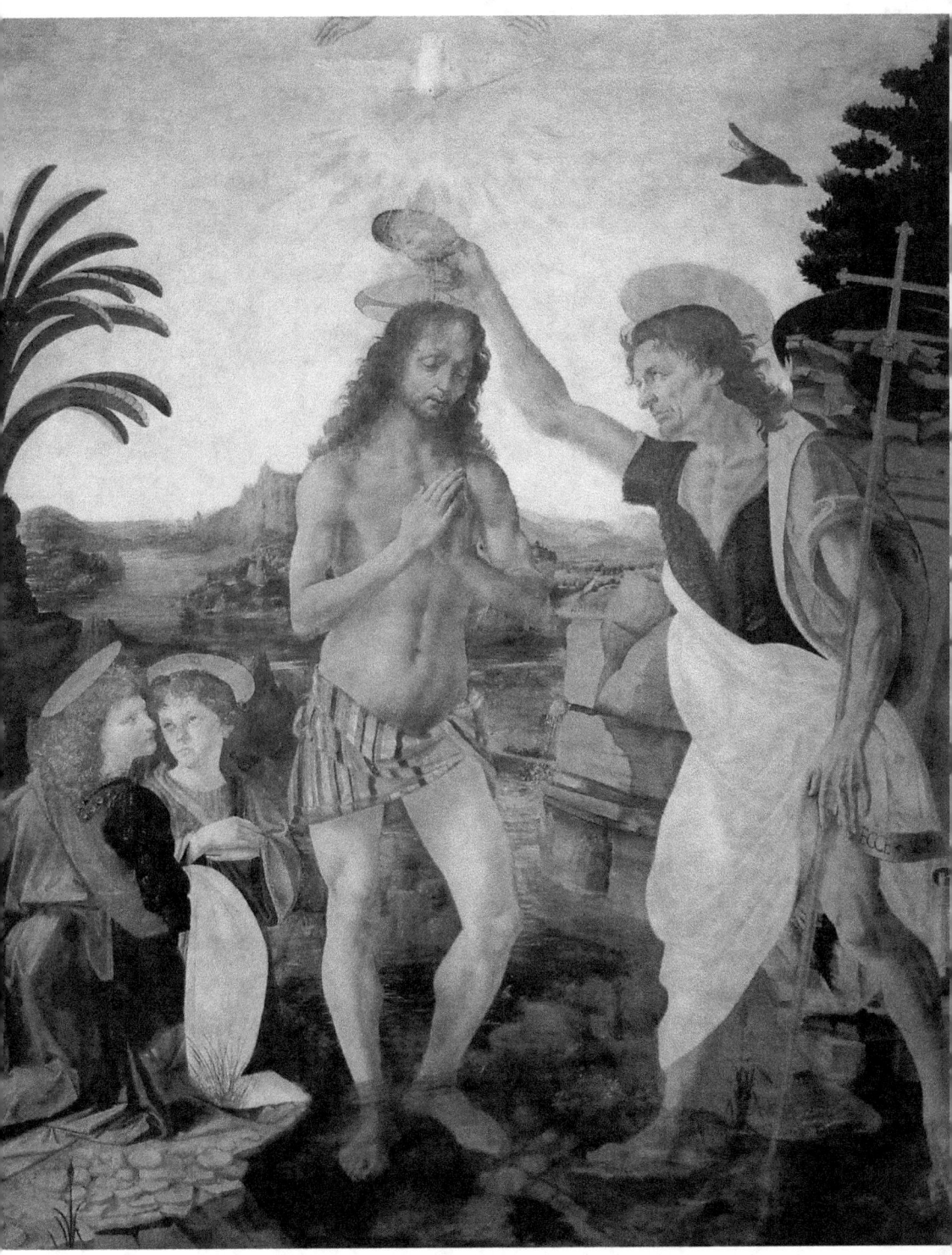

Andrea del Verrocchio, The Baptism of Christ

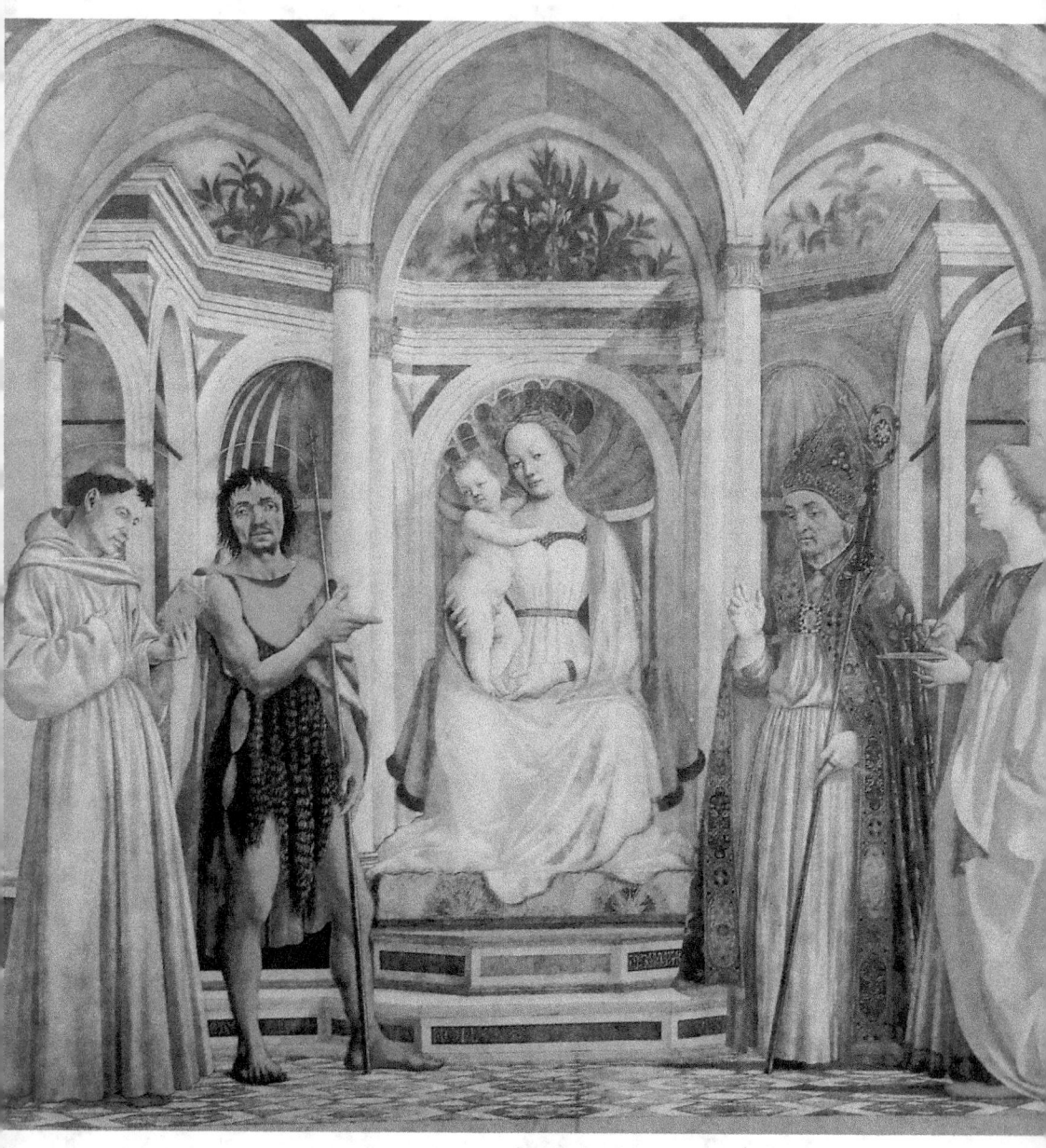

Domenico Veneziano, Madonna and Child With Saints, 1445, Uffizi Gallery

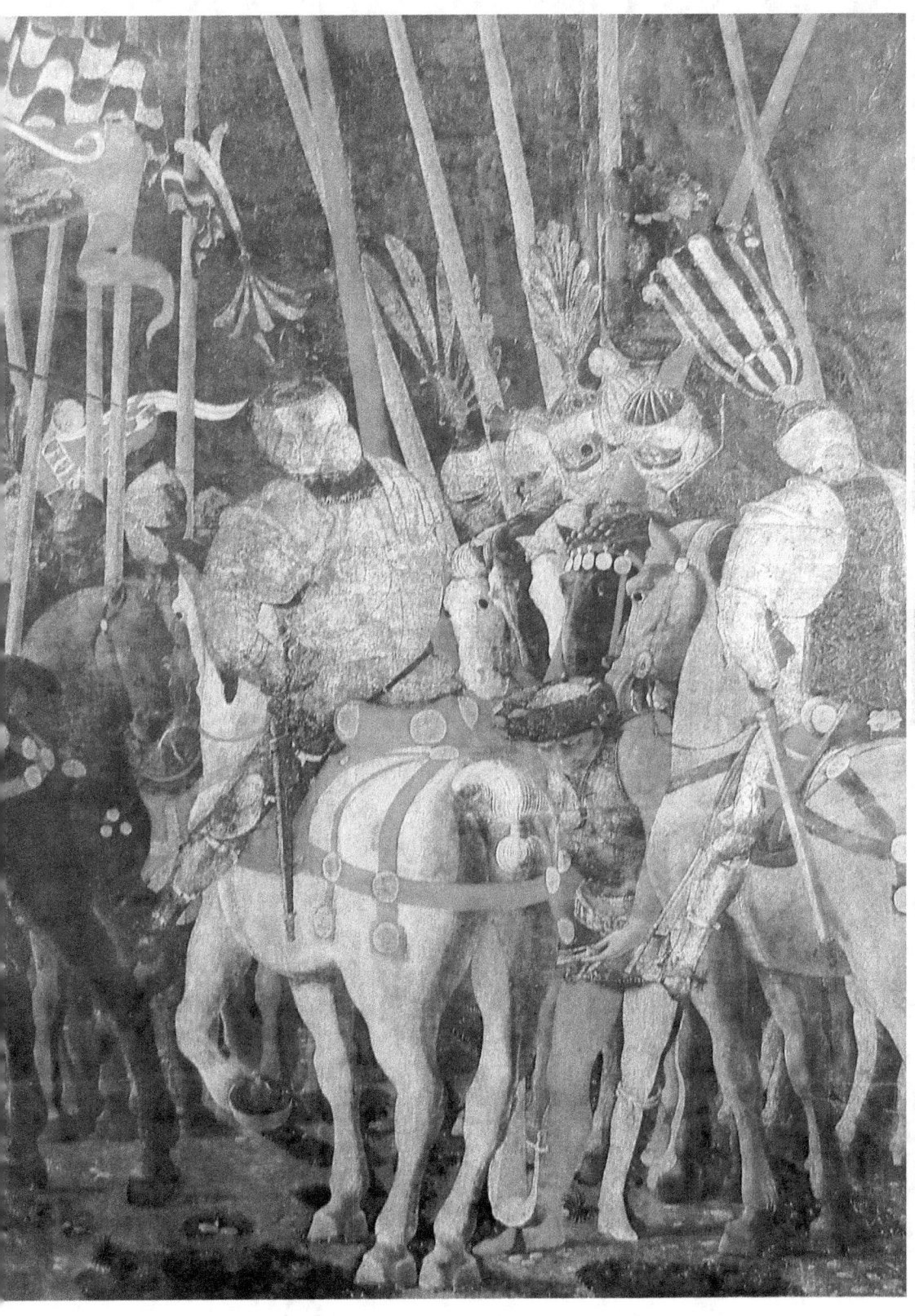

Paolo Uccello, Battle of San Romano, 1456-60, Loure, Paris

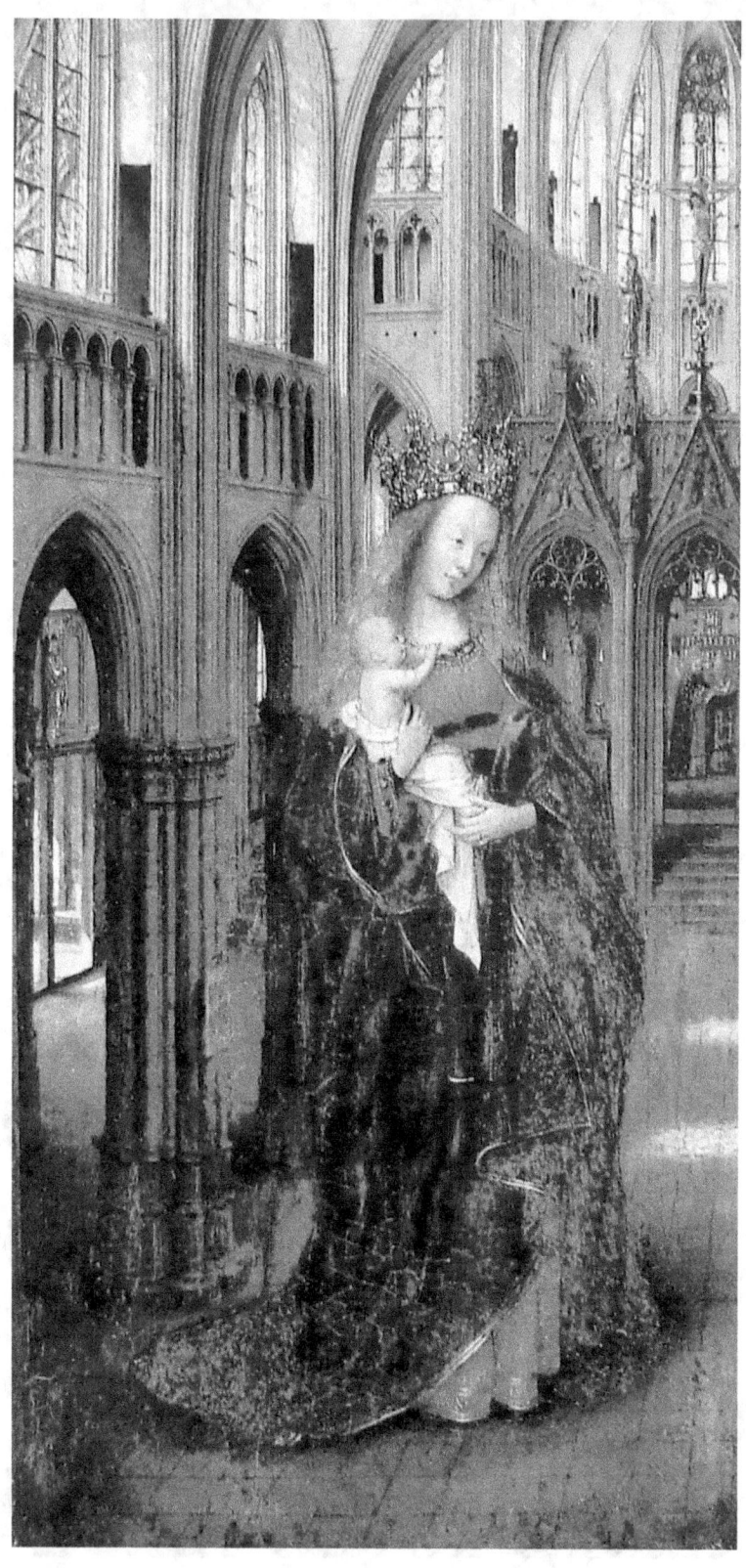

Jan van Eyck, Madonna In a Church, Berlin

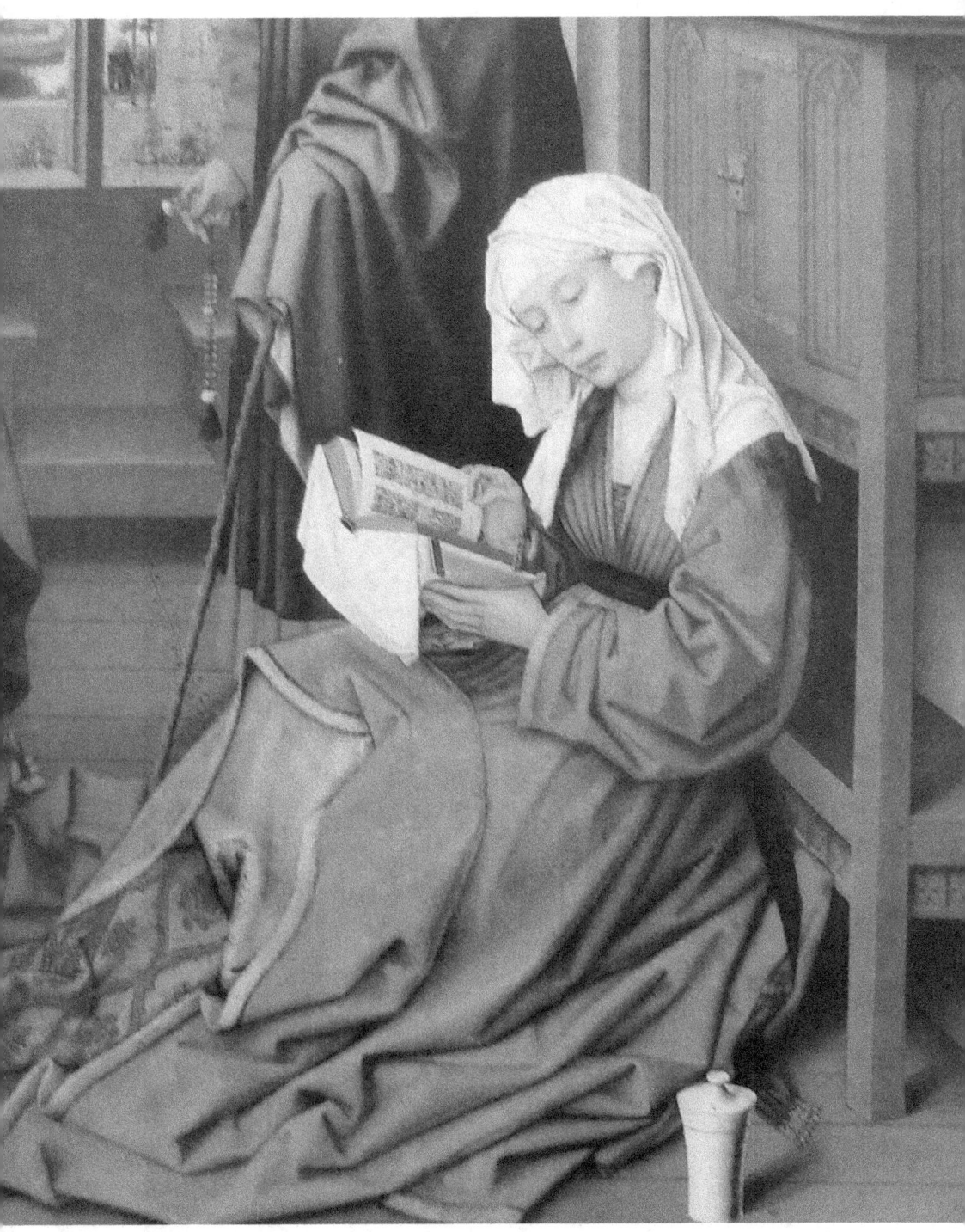

Rogier van der Weyden, Mary Magdalene Reading, detail, National Gallery, London

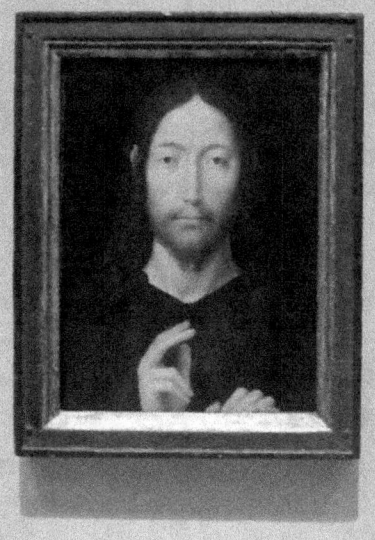
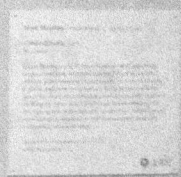

Hans Memling, Christ Blessing, Metropolitan Museum of Art

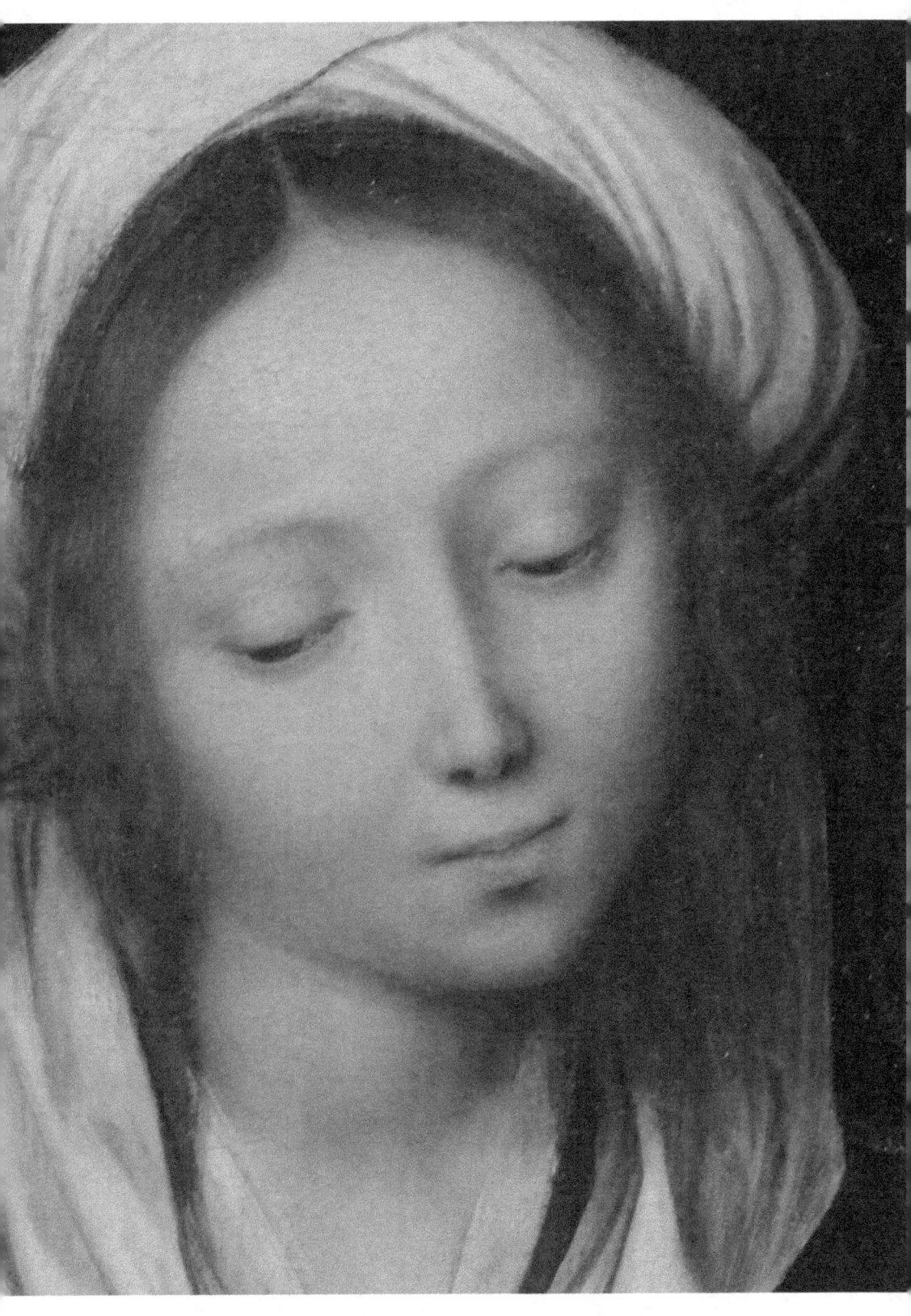

Gerard David, detail of the Adoration, Metropolitan Museum of Art

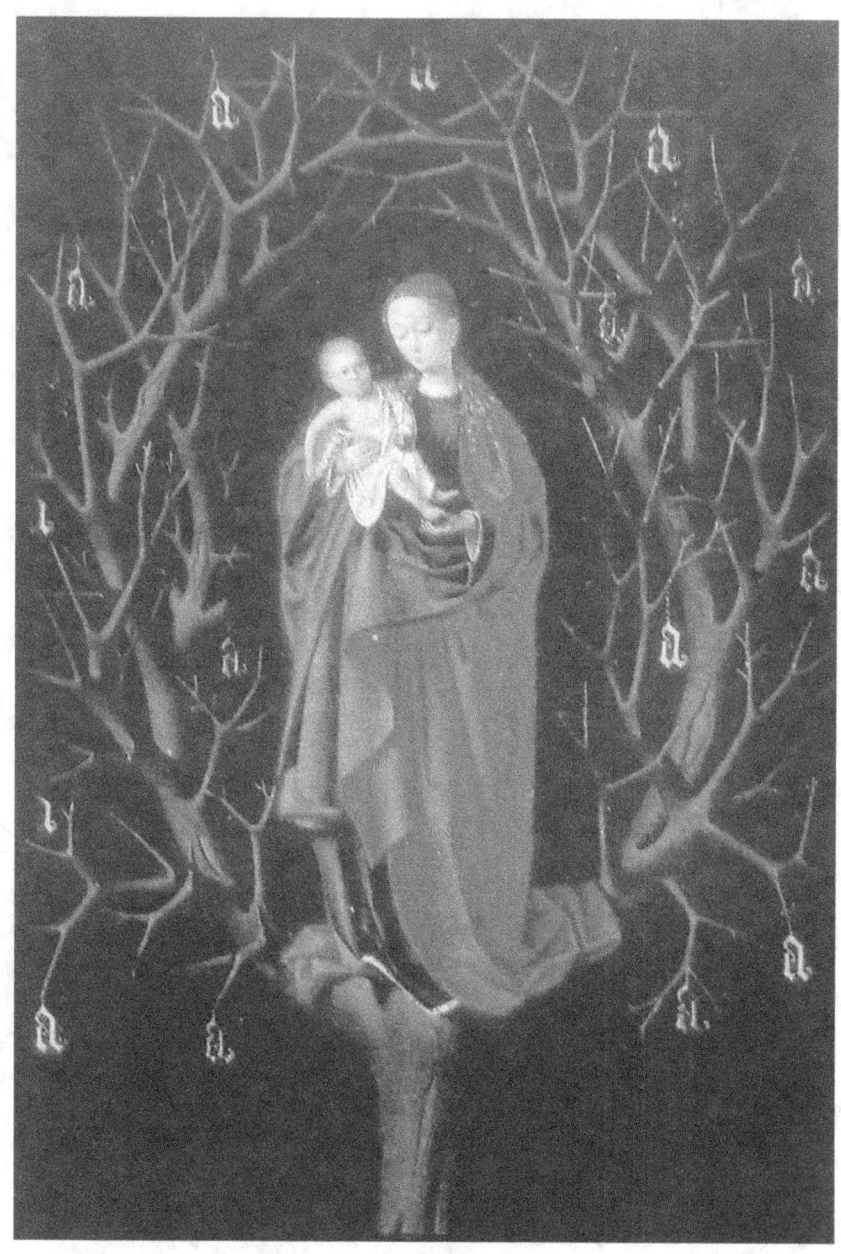

Petrus Christus, Madonna In a Barren Tree, 1450,
Prado, Madrid

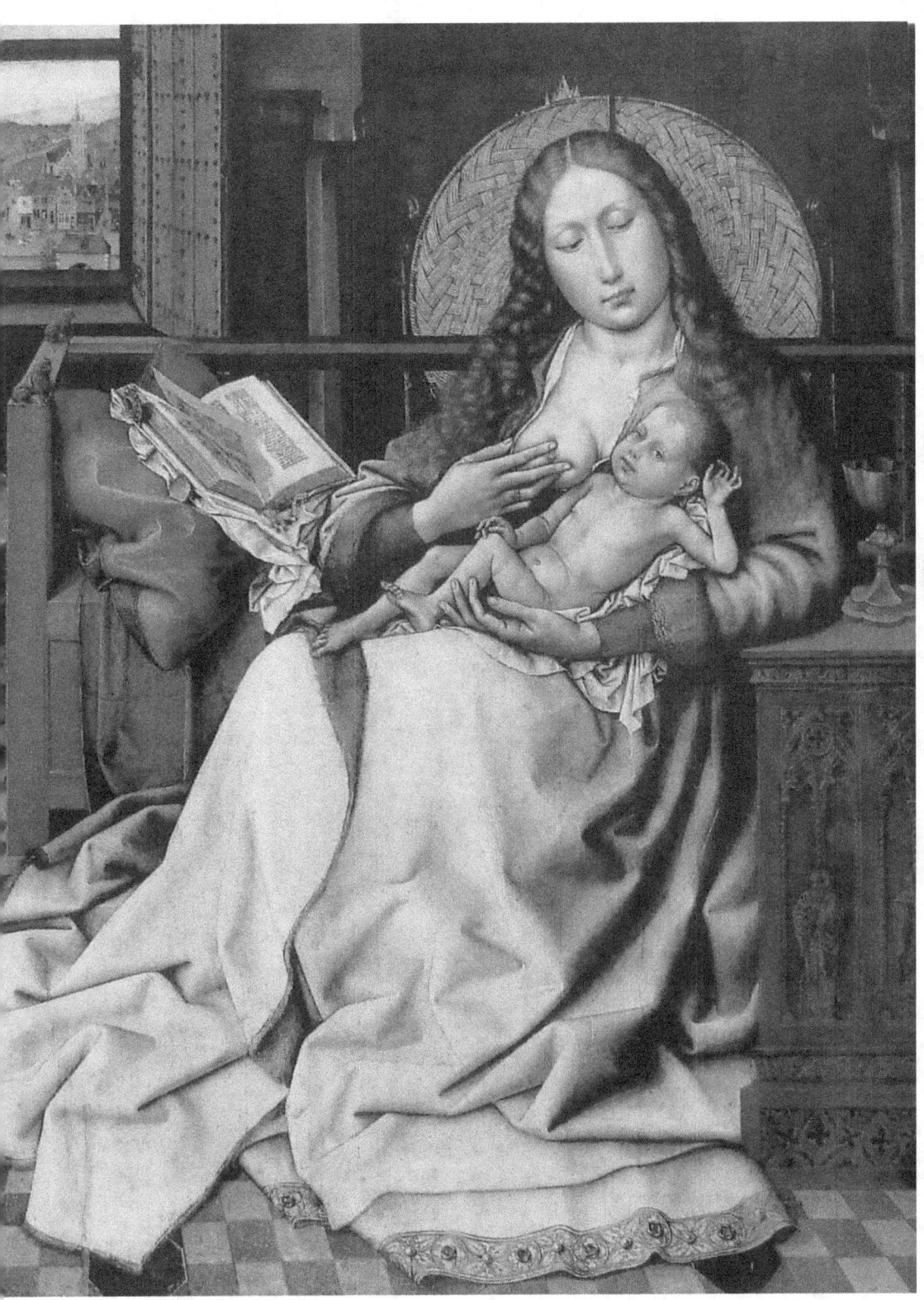

Robert Campin, Madonna With the Firescreen, National Gallery, London

Notes

I   *Fra Angelico and the Renaissance*

1   James Beck, 1981, 62
2   'In the cells of San Marco, insofar as it lay within his power to do so, he gave expression to the divine', writes G.C. Argan in *Fra Angelico* (10).
3   Christopher Lloyd writes in *Fra Angelico*: 'It needs to be emphasized his supreme qualities as a painter stem more from his mastery of style than from the sanctity of his subject matter.' (3)
4   Oswald Spengler says in *The Decline of the West* that 'the gold background [of painting] possesses, in the iconography of the western Church, an explicit dogmatic significance. It is an express assertion of the existence and activity of the divine spirit.' (140)
5   See Bruce Cole, 1983, 64.

II   *Fra Angelico as a Painter*

1   C. G. Jung: *Psychology and Religion: West and East*, Routledge & Kegan Paul 1971, 71.
2   See Philip Hendy: *Piero della Francesca and the Early Renaissance*, London 1968, 17.

III   *The Silent Annunciation*

1   Rainer Maria Rilke:

     Hail to thee, my soul beholds, thou art prepared and ripenest. Thou art a gateway great and high and thou shalt open soon. Thou, my song's dearest ear, now I feel: my word was lost in thee as in a wood.

(*The Book of Images*, tr. Edward Snow, North Point Press/ Farrar, Straus & Giroux, New York, 1994, 110-1).

2   Fra Roberto Caracciolo: *Sermones de Laudibus Sanctorum*, Naples 1489, in M. Baxandall, 1988, 51.

3   Fra Caracciolo, in M. Baxandall, 1988, 51-55.

4   Rainer Maria Rilke, *Translations From the Poetry of Rainer Maria Rilke*, tr. M.D. Herter Norton, W.W. Norton, 1993, 208-9.

5   In Ron Cameron: *The Other Gospels: Non-Canonical Gospel Texts*, Lutterworth Press, Surrey 1983, 141.

IV   *The Madonna in the Renaissance*

1   Julia Kristeva: "Motherhood According to Bellini", *Peinture*, December 1975, no 10-11, and in *The Kristeva Reader*, 1986, 243. Page numbers refer to this edition.

2   Chris Mihill: "Breast-feeding falls foul of men", *The Guardian*, 6 November 1993.

3   Andrea Dworkin: *Right-Wing Women: The Politics of Domesticated Females*, Women's Press 1983, 206.

4   J. Kristeva: "Extraterrestrials Suffering For Want of Love", in *Tales of Love*, 374.

VI   *Fra Angelico at San Marco, Florence*

1   R.M. Rilke: *Tagebücher aus der Frühzeit*, ed. Ernst Zinn, Frankfurt, 1973, 21-23; Donald Prater: *A Ringing Glass: The Life of Rainer Maria Rilke*, Clarendon Press 1994, 32, 45.

2   In *Fra Angelico*, Christopher Lloyd writes: 'The images are memorable because of their touching simplicity. Both the settings and the figures are restrained by a degree of objectivity which suggests that Christ's life is here being described, or merely recorded, rather than enacted.' (12)

3   Christopher Lloyd remarked in *Fra Angelico*: 'Few renderings of the Transfiguration are as challenging and as totally convincing as that painted in cell No. 6 at San Marco.' (12)

4   Mircea Eliade, September 1957, quoted in M. Eliade, 1988, xv.

5   Marina Warner writes in *Alone Of All Her Sex: The Myth and Cult of the Virgin Mary* of Fra Angelico's *Noli me tangere*: 'Fra Angelico caught the enigma and the majesty of their encounter in the garden on the walls of the convent of San Marco in Florence, where Christ majestically turns away with an ethereal gesture of disdain while Mary Magdalene kneels in worship before him.' (228)

Bibliography

I *On Fra Angelico*

G. C. Argan: *Fra Angelico*, Skira, Geneva 1955

U. Baldini: *Beato Angelico*, Edizioni d'Arte il Fiorino, Florence 1986

L. Berti et al: *Angelico at San Marco*, Sansoni, Florence 1965

M. OskovitsL "La fase tarda del Beato Angelico", *Arte cristiana*, LXXI, 1983, 11-24

—"Arte e formazione religosa – Il caso del Beato Angelico", in *L'uomo di fronte all'arte. Valori estetici e valori etico-religiosi*, La Spezia, 1985, *Vita e Pensiero*, 1986, 153-164

P. Cardile: "Fra Angelico's Shop at San Domenico in Fiesole", Ph. D thesis, Yale University 1974

G. Didi-Huberman: *Fra Angelico. Dissemblance et Figuration*, Flammarion, Paris 1990

—"La dissemblance des figures selon Fra Angelico", *Mélanges de l'Ecole Française de Rome. Moyn Age – Temps Moderne*, XCVIII, 1986, 709-802

D. Dini & G. Bonsanti: "Fra Angelico e gli affreschi nel Convento di San Marco (ca. 1441-50)", in E. Borsook & F. Superbi Gioffredi, ed. *Tecnica e Stile. Esempi di pittura murale del Rinascimento italiano*, Harvard Center for Italian Renaissance Studies at Villa I Tatti, 1986, 17-24

A. Francini Ciaranfi: *Beato Angelico: Gli affreschi di San Marco*, Amilcare Pizzi S. p. A, Milan 1940

C. Gilbert: "A Sign about Signing in a Fresco by Fra Angelico", in *Tribute to Lotte Brand Philip*, Abaris Books, New York 1985, 65-70

—"Fra Angeloc", *Theologische Realenzyklopädie*, II, 5, Waler de Gruyter, Berlin, 19978, 710-3

—"The Conversion of Fra Angelico", in *Scritti di Storia dell'Arte in onore di Roberto Salvini*, ed. C. De Benedictis, G.C. Sansoni Editore Nuova,

Florence 1984, 281-7

A. Hertz: *Fra Angelico,* Edizioni Paoline, Rome 1983

William Hood: *Fra Angelico at San Marco,* Yale University Press, New Haven 1993

—"Fra Angelico at San Marco: Art and the Liturgy of Cloistered Life", in T. Verdon & J. Henderson, eds. *Christianity and the Renaissance,* Syracuse University Press, Syracuse 1990, 108-131

—"St Dominic's Manners of Praying: Gestures in Fra Angelico's Frescoes at S. Marco", *Art Bulletin,* LXVIII, 1986, 195-206

P. Joannides: "Fra Angelico: Two Annunciations", *Arte cristiana,* LXXVII, 1989, 303-308

R. Krautheimer: "Fra Angelico and - perhaps - Alberti", in J. Plummer & I. Lavin, eds. *Studies in Late Medieval and Renaissance Painting Presented to Millard Meiss,* New York University Press, New York 1977, 290-296

A. Ladis: "Fra Angelico: newly discovered document from the 1420s", *Mitteilungen des Kunsthistorischen Institutes in Florenz,* XXV, 1981, 378-9

Christopher Lloyd: *Fra Angelico,* Phaidon 1979

S. Madigan: "A New Interpretation of the Iconography of Fra Angelico: Rosarian Organization in the Frescoed Cells of San Marco", MACAA paper, Hamlite University, St Paul, 1977

J. Miller: "Medici Patronage and the Iconography of Fra Angelico's San Marco Altarpiece", *Studies in Iconography,* XI, 1987, 1-13

S. Orlandi: *Beato Angelico,* Leo S. Olscki, Florence 1964

John Pope-Hennessy: *Fra Angelico,* Phaidon 1974

U. Procacci: "Recent restoration in Florence, II: Fra Angelico, Sassetta and others", *Burlington Magazine,* LXXXIX, 1947, 330-4

M. Salmi: *Beato Angelico,* Edizioni Valori Plastici, Rome 1958

P. Sheaffer: "White Light and Meditation at San Marco", *Memorie Domenicane,* XIV, 1983, 329-334

I. Strunk: *Fra Angelico aus dem Dominikanerorden,* B. Kuehlens Kunstanstalt u. Verlag, Gladbach 1916

II   *Renaissance and General Works*

C.G. Argan: *The Renaissance*, Thames & Hudson 1969

Karen Armstrong: *The Gospel According to Woman; Christianity's Creation of the Sex War in the West*, Pan 1987

Karen Arthurs: *A Survey of the Notions Behind, and the Mechanics of, Harmony Within the Composition of Art From Prehistory to the Renaissance*, BA thesis, Newcastle Polytechnic 1984

Geoffrey Ashe: *The Virgin: Mary's Cult and the Re-emergence of the Goddess*, Arkana 1987

—*Discovering the Goddess: A Personal Testimony*, Crescent Moon 1995

Michael Baxandall: *Painting and Experience in 15th Century Italy*, Oxford University Press 1988

—*Patterns of Intention: On the Historical Explanation of Pictures*, Yale University Press 1985

James Beck: *Italian Renaissance Painting*, Harper & Row, New York 1981

Ean Begg: *The Cult of the Black Virgin*, Routledge 1985

Stephan Beissel. *Fra Angelico (Temporis Collection)*, Parkstone Press, 2007

Bernard Berenson: *The Italian Painters of the Renaissance*, Phaidon, 1952

—*Looking at Pictures with Bernard Berenson*, selected by Hann Kiel, Abrahams, New York 1974

Pamela Berger: *The Goddess Obscured*, Robert Hale 1988

Bruce Bernard: *The Queen of Heaven: A Selection of Painting the Virgin from the Twelfth to the Eighteenth Centuries*, Macdonald/ Orbis 1987

—*The Bible and Its Painters*, Orbis 1983

Botticelli: *The Complete Paintings of Botticelli*, Granada 1980

Charles Bouleau: *The Painter's Secret Geometry: A Study of Composition in Art*, tr. Jonathan Griffin, Thames & Hudson 1963

Serge Bramly: *Leonardo: The Artist and the Man*, Michael Joseph 1992

Allan Brahama: *Italian Renaissance Painters of the Sixteenth Century*, National Gallery 1985

Helmut Brinker: *Zen in the Art of Painting*, Routledge & Kegan Paul 1987

Stephanie Brown: *Religious Painting*, Phaidon 1979

Francesco Buranelli and Collectif. *Fra Angelico: la chapelle niccoline du Vatican: Histoire et restauration*, 2003

Jacob Burckhardt: *The Altarpiece in Renaissance Italy*, Phaidon 1988

Titus Burckhardt: *Sacred Art in East and West*, Perennial Book, Middlesex 1967

Ritchie Calder: *Leonardo and The Age of the Eye*, Heinemann 1970

Joseph Campbell: *The Power of Myth*, with Bill Moyers, ed. Betty Sue Flowers, Doubleday, New York 1988

Michael P. Carroll: *The Cult of the Virgin Mary*, Princeton University

Press, New Jersey 1986

Julia Cartwright. *The Painters of Florence*, London, 1865

Richard Cavendish: *Visions of Heaven and Hell*, Orbis 1977

Andre Chastel: *Art of the Italian Renaissance*, tr. Peter & Linda Murray, Alpine Fine Arts Collection 1985

— *The Studios and Styles of the Renaissance, Italy 1460-1500*, tr. Griffin, Thames & Hudson 1966

Hugo Chapman and Marzia Faietti. *Fra Angelico to Leonardo: Italian Renaissance Drawings*, 2010

Herschel B. Chipp, ed. *Theories of Modern Art*, University Press of California, Los Angeles 1968

Bruce Cole: *The Renaissance Artist at Work*, John Murray 1983

Charles D. Cuttler: *Northern Painting From Pucelle to Bruegel*, Holt, Rinehart & Winston, New York 1968

Georges Didi-Huberman. *Fra Angelico: Dissemblance and Figuration*, 1995

Robert Langton Douglas. *Fra Angelico*, 2009

Lene Dresen-Coenders, ed. *Saints and She-Devils: Images of Women in the 15th and 16th Centuries*, Rubicon Press 1987

Andrea Dworkin: *Intercourse*, Arrow 1988

Donald Ehresmann: "Some Observations on the Role of the Liturgy in the Early Winged Altarpiece", *Art Bulletin*, LXIV, 1982

Colin Eisler: *Early Netherlandish Painting: The Thyssen-Bornemisza Collection*, Sotheby's Publications 1989

Mircea Eliade: *Ordeal by Labyrinth*, University of Chicago Press 1984

— *Symbolism, the Sacred and the Arts*, Crossroad, New York 1985

Joan Evans, ed. *The Flowering of the Middle Ages*, Thames & Hudson 1966

Giorgio T. Faggin: *The Complete Paintings of the Van Eycks*, Wiedenfeld & Nicolson 1970

John Fletcher & Andrew Benjamin, ed; *Abjection, Melancholia and Love: the Work of Julia Kristeva*, Routledge 1990

S.J. Freedberg: *Painting of the High Renaissance in Rome and Florence*, Harper & Row, New York 1972

Sigmund Freud: *Leonardo da Vinci*, tr. Alan Tyson, Penguin 1963

Max J. Friedlander: *From Van Eyck to Bruegel*, Phaidon 1969

— *The van Eycks, Petrus Christus*, Early Netherlandish Painting vol. 1, tr. Heinz Norden, Sijthoff, Leyden, Netherlands 1967

Eugène Fromentin: *The Masters of Past Time: Dutch and Flemish Painting from Van Eyck to Rembrandt*, Phaidon 1981

Niny Garavaghlia: *The Complete Paintings of Mantegna*, Weidenfeld & Nicholson 1971

Fred Gettings: *The Hidden Art: A Study of the Occult Symbolism in Art*, Studio Vista 1978

Matila Ghyka: *The Geometry of Art and Life*, Sheed & Ward, New York 1946

Marija Gimbutas: *The Language of the Goddess*, Thames & Hudson 1989

Rona Goffen: *Giovanni Bellini*, Yale University Press, New Haven 1989

Robert Goldwater & Marco Treves, eds. *Artists on Art*, John Murray 1975

E.H. Gombrich: *Norm and Form: Studies in the Renaissance I*, Phaidon 1985

— *Symbolic Images, Renaissance Studies II*, Phaidon 1985

Thomas G. Goodwin. *The Life of Fra Angelico Da Fiesole*, 2009

Cecil Gould: *Leonardo: The Artist and the Non-Artist*, Weidenfeld & Nicholson 1975

—"On the Direction of Light in Italian Renaissance Frescoes and Altarpieces", *Gazette des Beaux-Arts*, 6, XCVII, 1981

John Hale: *Italian Renaissance Painting*, Phaidon 1977

James Hall: *A Dictionary of Subjects and Symbols in Art*, John Murray 1984

Frederick Hartt: *History of Italian Renaissance Art: Painting, Sculpture, Architecture*, Thomas & Hudson 1987

— *Sandro Botticelli*, Collins 1954

P. Jolly: "Rogier van der Weyden's Escorial and Philadelphia *Crucifixions* and their relation to Fra Angelico at San Marco", *Oud Holland*, XCV, 1981, 113-126

Laurence B. Kanter. *Rediscovering Fra Angelico*, Metropolitan Museum of Art, 2001

Julia Kristeva: *The Kristeva Reader*, ed. Toril Moi, Blackwell 1986

— *Desire in Language: A Semiotic Approach to Literature and Art*, ed. Leon Roudiez, tr. Thomas Gora, Alice Jardine & Leon Roudiez, Blackwell 1982

Weston La Barre: *The Ghost Dance*, Allen & Unwin 1972

Barbara Lane: *The Altar and the Altarpiece: Sacramental Themes in Early Netherlandish Painting*, New York 1984

—"Sacred vs Profane in Early Netherlandish Painting", *Simiolus*, XVIII, 1988

Leonardo da Vinci: *The Drawings of Leonardo da Vinci*, introduction A.E. Popham, Cape, 1964

— *Selections from the Notebooks*, Oxford University Press 1952

Michael Levey: *High Renaissance*, Penguin 1975

— *Early Renaissance*, Penguin 1967

Robert Longhi: *Piero della Francesca*, Milan 1955

Elaine Marks & Isabelle de Courtivron, eds. *New French Feminisms: an Anthology*, Harvester Wheatsheaf 1981

G. Marchini: *Filippo Lippi*, Electa Editrice, Milan 1975

Domenico Marcucci and Edmund C. Lane. *The Rosary with Fra Angelico and Giotto*, 2005

James Marrow: "Symbol and Meaning in Northern European Art of the Late Middle Ages and Early Renaissance", *Simiolus*, XVI, 1986

Milliard Meiss: "Light as Form and Symbol in Some Fifteenth Century Paintings", *Art Bulletin*, XXVII, 1945

J.C.J. Metford: *Dictionary of Christian Lore and Legend*, Thames & Hudson 1983

Edward Mullins: *The Painted Witch: Female Body, Male Art*, Secker & Warburg 1985

Linda Murray: *High Renaissance*, Thames & Hudson 1977

Lynda Nead: *Female Nude: Art, Obscenity and Sexuality*, Routledge 1992

Erich Neumann: *The Great Mother*, Princeton University Press, New Jersey 1972

Shirley Nicholson, ed. *The Goddess Re-awakening: The Goddess Principle Today* Theosophical Publishing House, New York 1989

Rudolf Otto: *The Idea of the Holy*, Oxford University Press 1958

Erwin Panofsky: *Studies in Iconology*, Harper & Row, New York 1972

— *Early Netherlandish Painting*, Harvard University Press, Mass., 1953

Walter Pater: *The Renaissance*, Oxford University Press 1980

Michael Payne: *Reading Theory: An Introduction to Lacan, Derrida, and Kristeva*, Blackwell 1993

Robert Payne: *Leonardo da Vinci*, Robert hale 1979

C. Purtle: *The Marian Paintings of Jan van Eyck*, Princeton University Press, Princeton 1982

Kathleen J. Reiger, ed. *The Spiritual Image in Modern Art*, Theosophical Publishing House, Wheaton, Illinois 1987

D. Robb: "The Iconography of the Annunciation in the Fourteenth and Fifteenth Centuries", *Art Bulletin*, XVIII, 1936, 480-526

John Ruskin: *Works*, ed. E.T.Cook & A. Wedderburn, 39 vols, Allen 1903-12

Monica Sjöo & Barbara Mor: *The Great Cosmic Mother*, Harper & Row, San Francisco 1987

Alistair Smith: *Early Netherlandish and German Painting*, National Gallery 1985

J. Spencer: "Spatial Imagery of the Annunciation in Fifteenth-century Florence", *Art Bulletin*, XXXVI, 1955, 273-280

Oswald Spengler: *The Decline of the West*, Allen & Unwin 1961

Wolfgang Stechow: *Northern Renaissance Art, 1400-1600, Sources and Documents*, Prentice-Hall, New Jersey 1966

L. Steinberg & S. Edgerton: "How shall this be? Reflections on Filippo Lippi's *Annunciation* in London", *Artibus et Historiæ*, VIII, 1987, 25-53

Victor I. Stoichita: *Leonardo da Vinci*, Abbey Library 1978

Moses Foster Sweetser. *Artist-Biographies: Fra Angelico*, 2008

H. F. Ullman. *Fra Angelico (Masters of Art)*, 2007

Nicholas Usherwood: *The Bible in 20th Century Art*, Pagoda Books 1987

Lionello Venturi: *Renaissance Painting, from Leonardo to Dürer*, Skira/Macmillan 1979

— *Italian Paintings*, Zwemmer 1950

— *Botticelli*, Phaidon 1964

Marina Warner: *Alone Of All Her Sex: The Myth and Cult of the Virgin Mary*, Picador 1985
— *Monuments and Maidens*, Weidenfeld & Nicholson 1985
Margaret Whinney: *Early Flemish Painters*, Faber 1966
John White: *The Birth and Rebirth of Pictorial Space*, Faber 1957/87
Peter Lamborn Wilson: *Angels*, Thames & Hudson 1980
Heinrich Wolfflin: *Classic Art*, Phaidon 1952/80
Marion Woodman: *The Pregnant Virgin: A Process of Psychological Transformation*, Inner City Books, Toronto 1989
Manfred Wudram: *Art of the Renaissance*, Weidenfeld & Nicolson 1985
J.E. Zeigler: "The Medieval Virgin as Object: Art of Anthropology?", *Historical Reflections*, XVI, 1989
Charles Zika: "Hosts, Processions and Pilgrimages: Controlling the Sacred in Fifteenth-Century Germany", *Past and Present*, CXVIII, 1988

CRESCENT MOON PUBLISHING

ARTS, PAINTING, SCULPTURE

The Art of Andy Goldsworthy
Andy Goldsworthy: Touching Nature
Andy Goldsworthy in Close-Up
Andy Goldsworthy: Pocket Guide
Andy Goldsworthy In America
Land Art: A Complete Guide
The Art of Richard Long
Richard Long: Pocket Guide
Land Art In the UK
Land Art in Close-Up
Land Art In the U.S.A.
Land Art: Pocket Guide
Installation Art in Close-Up
Minimal Art and Artists In the 1960s and After
Colourfield Painting
Land Art DVD, TV documentary
Andy Goldsworthy DVD, TV documentary
The Erotic Object: Sexuality in Sculpture From Prehistory to the Present Day
Sex in Art: Pornography and Pleasure in Painting and Sculpture
Postwar Art
Sacred Gardens: The Garden in Myth, Religion and Art
Glorification: Religious Abstraction in Renaissance and 20th Century Art
Early Netherlandish Painting
Leonardo da Vinci
Piero della Francesca
Giovanni Bellini
Fra Angelico: Art and Religion in the Renaissance
Mark Rothko: The Art of Transcendence
Frank Stella: American Abstract Artist
Jasper Johns
Brice Marden
Alison Wilding: The Embrace of Sculpture
Vincent van Gogh: Visionary Landscapes
Eric Gill: Nuptials of God
Constantin Brancusi: Sculpting the Essence of Things
Max Beckmann
Caravaggio
Gustave Moreau
Egon Schiele: Sex and Death In Purple Stockings
Delizioso Fotografico Fervore: Works In Process 1
Sacro Cuore: Works In Process 2
The Light Eternal: J.M.W. Turner
The Madonna Glorified: Karen Arthurs

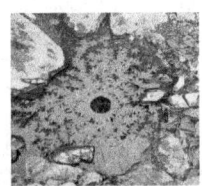
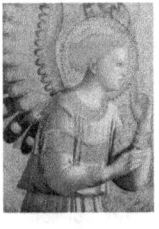
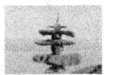
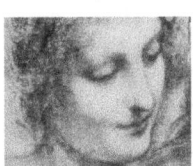
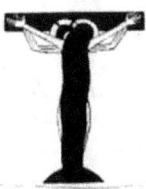
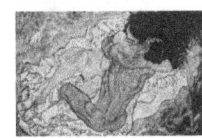

LITERATURE

J.R.R. Tolkien: The Books, The Films, The Whole Cultural Phenomenon
J.R.R. Tolkien: Pocket Guide
Tolkien's Heroic Quest
The *Earthsea* Books of Ursula Le Guin
Beauties, Beasts and Enchantment: Classic French Fairy Tales
German Popular Stories by the Brothers Grimm
Philip Pullman and *His Dark Materials*
Sexing Hardy: Thomas Hardy and Feminism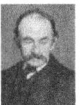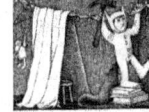
Thomas Hardy's *Tess of the d'Urbervilles*
Thomas Hardy's *Jude the Obscure*
Thomas Hardy: The Tragic Novels
Love and Tragedy: Thomas Hardy
The Poetry of Landscape in Hardy
Wessex Revisited: Thomas Hardy and John Cowper Powys
Wolfgang Iser: Essays and Interviews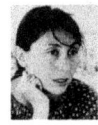
Petrarch, Dante and the Troubadours
Maurice Sendak and the Art of Children's Book Illustration
Andrea Dworkin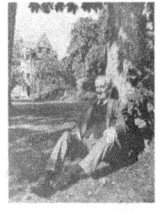
Cixous, Irigaray, Kristeva: The *Jouissance* of French Feminism
Julia Kristeva: Art, Love, Melancholy, Philosophy, Semiotics and Psychoanalysis
Hélène Cixous I Love You: The *Jouissance* of Writing
Luce Irigaray: Lips, Kissing, and the Politics of Sexual Difference
Peter Redgrove: Here Comes the Flood
Peter Redgrove: Sex-Magic-Poetry-Cornwall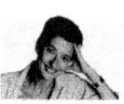
Lawrence Durrell: Between Love and Death, East and West
Love, Culture & Poetry: Lawrence Durrell
Cavafy: Anatomy of a Soul
German Romantic Poetry: Goethe, Novalis, Heine, Hölderlin
Feminism and Shakespeare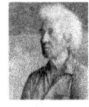
Shakespeare: Love, Poetry & Magic
The Passion of D.H. Lawrence
D.H. Lawrence: Symbolic Landscapes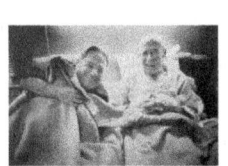
D.H. Lawrence: Infinite Sensual Violence
Rimbaud: Arthur Rimbaud and the Magic of Poetry
The Ecstasies of John Cowper Powys
Sensualism and Mythology: The Wessex Novels of John Cowper Powys
Amorous Life: John Cowper Powys and the Manifestation of Affectivity (H.W. Fawkner)
Postmodern Powys: New Essays on John Cowper Powys (Joe Boulter)
Rethinking Powys: Critical Essays on John Cowper Powys
Paul Bowles & Bernardo Bertolucci
Rainer Maria Rilke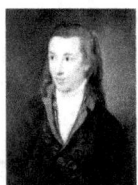
Joseph Conrad: *Heart of Darkness*
In the Dim Void: Samuel Beckett
Samuel Beckett Goes into the Silence
André Gide: Fiction and Fervour
Jackie Collins and the Blockbuster Novel
Blinded By Her Light: The Love-Poetry of Robert Graves
The Passion of Colours: Travels In Mediterranean Lands
Poetic Forms

POETRY

Ursula Le Guin: Walking In Cornwall
Peter Redgrove: Here Comes The Flood
Peter Redgrove: Sex-Magic-Poetry-Cornwall
Dante: Selections From the Vita Nuova
Petrarch, Dante and the Troubadours
William Shakespeare: Sonnets
William Shakespeare: Complete Poems
Blinded By Her Light: The Love-Poetry of Robert Graves
Emily Dickinson: Selected Poems
Emily Brontë: Poems
Thomas Hardy: Selected Poems
Percy Bysshe Shelley: Poems
John Keats: Selected Poems
Joh n Keats: Poems of 1820
D.H. Lawrence: Selected Poems
Edmund Spenser: Poems
Edmund Spenser: Amoretti
John Donne: Poems
Henry Vaughan: Poems
Sir Thomas Wyatt: Poems
Robert Herrick: Selected Poems
Rilke: Space, Essence and Angels in the Poetry of Rainer Maria Rilke
Rainer Maria Rilke: Selected Poems
Friedrich Hölderlin: Selected Poems
Arseny Tarkovsky: Selected Poems
Arthur Rimbaud: Selected Poems
Arthur Rimbaud: A Season in Hell
Arthur Rimbaud and the Magic of Poetry
Novalis: Hymns To the Night
German Romantic Poetry
Paul Verlaine: Selected Poems
Elizaethan Sonnet Cycles
D.J. Enright: By-Blows
Jeremy Reed: Brigitte's Blue Heart
Jeremy Reed: Claudia Schiffer's Red Shoes
Gorgeous Little Orpheus
Radiance: New Poems
Crescent Moon Book of Nature Poetry
Crescent Moon Book of Love Poetry
Crescent Moon Book of Mystical Poetry
Crescent Moon Book of Elizabethan Love Poetry
Crescent Moon Book of Metaphysical Poetry
Crescent Moon Book of Romantic Poetry
Pagan America: New American Poetry

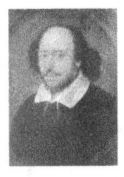
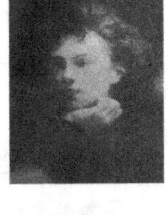
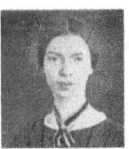
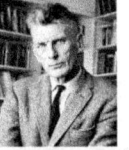
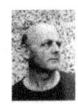
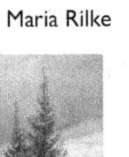
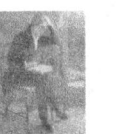
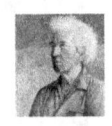
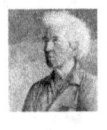
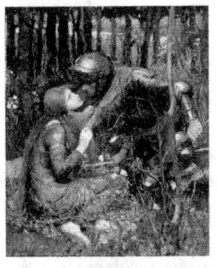
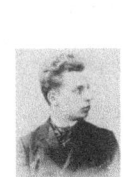
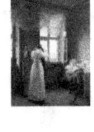
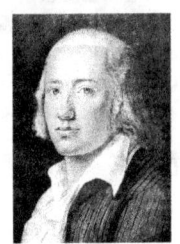
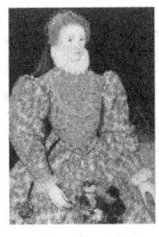

J.R.R. Tolkien: The Books, The Films, The Whole Cultural Phenomenon
J.R.R. Tolkien: Pocket Guide
The *Lord of the Rings* Movies: Pocket Guide
The Cinema of Hayao Miyazaki
Hayao Miyazaki: *Princess Mononoke*: Pocket Movie Guide
Hayao Miyazaki: *Spirited Away*: Pocket Movie Guide
Tim Burton
Ken Russell
Ken Russell: *Tommy*: Pocket Movie Guide
The Ghost Dance: The Origins of Religion
The Peyote Cult
Cixous, Irigaray, Kristeva: The *Jouissance* of French Feminism
Julia Kristeva: Art, Love, Melancholy, Philosophy, Semiotics and Psychoanalysis
Luce Irigaray: Lips, Kissing, and the Politics of Sexual Difference
Hélène Cixous I Love You: The *Jouissance* of Writing
Andrea Dworkin
'Cosmo Woman': The World of Women's Magazines
Women in Pop Music
Discovering the Goddess (Geoffrey Ashe)
The Poetry of Cinema
The Sacred Cinema of Andrei Tarkovsky
Andrei Tarkovsky: Pocket Guide
Andrei Tarkovsky: *Mirror*: Pocket Movie Guide
Andrei Tarkovsky: *The Sacrifice*: Pocket Movie Guide
Walerian Borowczyk: Cinema of Erotic Dreams
Jean-Luc Godard: The Passion of Cinema
Jean-Luc Godard: *Hail Mary*: Pocket Movie Guide
Jean-Luc Godard: *Contempt*: Pocket Movie Guide
Jean-Luc Godard: *Pierrot le Fou*: Pocket Movie Guide
John Hughes and Eighties Cinema
Ferris Bueller's Day Off: Pocket Movie Guide
Jean-Luc Godard: Pocket Guide
The Cinema of Richard Linklater
Liv Tyler: Star In Ascendance
Blade Runner and the Films of Philip K. Dick
Paul Bowles and Bernardo Bertolucci
Media Hell: Radio, TV and the Press
An Open Letter to the BBC
Detonation Britain: Nuclear War in the UK
Feminism and Shakespeare
Wild Zones: Pornography, Art and Feminism
Sex in Art: Pornography and Pleasure in Painting and Sculpture
Sexing Hardy: Thomas Hardy and Feminism

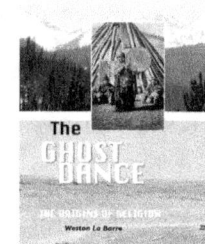
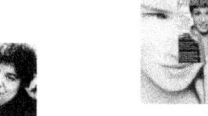
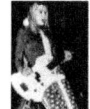
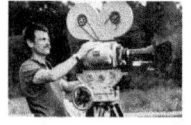
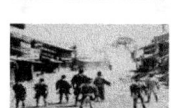
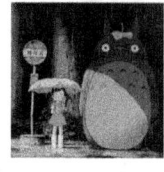
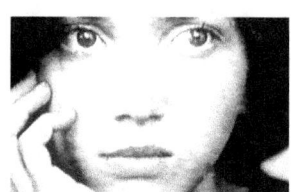

In my view *The Light Eternal* is among the very best of all the material I read on Turner. (Douglas Graham, director of the Turner Museum, Denver, Colorado)

The Light Eternal is a model monograph, an exemplary job. The subject matter of the book is beautifully organised and dead on beam. (Lawrence Durrell)

It is amazing for me to see my work treated with such passion and respect. (Andrea Dworkin)

CRESCENT MOON PUBLISHING
P.O. Box 1312, Maidstone, Kent, ME14 5XU, Great Britain. www.crmoon.com

www.ingramcontent.com/pod-product-compliance
Lightning Source LLC
Chambersburg PA
CBHW051317220526
45468CB00004B/1385